"Jim Elliott"

Shadow of the
ALMIGHTY

LifeSkills for Men

Also of Interest

9604

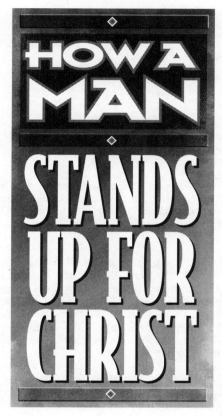

JIM GILBERT

DAVID HAZARD, *General Editor*

BETHANY HOUSE PUBLISHERS
MINNEAPOLIS, MINNESOTA 55438

Published by Bethany House Publishers
A Ministry of Bethany Fellowship, Inc.
11300 Hampshire Avenue South
Minneapolis, Minnesota 55438

Printed in the United States of America.

Library of Congress Cataloging-in-Publication Data

Gilbert, Jim.
    How a man stands up for Christ / Jim Gilbert.
        p.   cm. — (Lifeskills for men)
    ISBN 1–55661–844–1
    1. Men—Religious life. 2. Witness bearing (Christianity)
3. Evangelistic work. I. Title. II. Series.
BV4528.2.G55   1996
248.8'42—dc20   96–10067
                                                     CIP

To my parents

who taught me how to stand

and

To Dolly

who always stands beside me.

Jim Gilbert is Founder and President of the Nehemiah Project, as well as producer of the Rebuilder Video Schools, a local church-based video curriculum designed to impart practical skills and a biblical worldview to new believers, especially those in Eastern Bloc countries. He has also composed a variety of songs, and recorded four albums, including Integrity's Hosanna! Music release "Lamb of God." Jim and his wife, Dolly, live in Clearwater, Florida.

Acknowledgments

I owe the deepest gratitude to several people without whom this book could not have been written.

Chief among them is my remarkable and wonderful wife, Dolly, who graciously and without complaint took upon her already overburdened back the full weight of running The Nehemiah Project, our missions ministry, while I was hunched over my laptop discovering how much I loved to write. Darling, I never meant for your name to become a job description.

Profuse thanks also to David Hazard, who created a monster when he encouraged me to write. A superb editor and even more superb friend, he will never be forgiven by my wife.

I was a freshman at Oral Roberts University when seniors Terry Law and Larry Dalton invited me to join them and ten other students in forming a team that would combine contemporary music with straightforward preaching in weekend evangelistic outreaches for the rest of the spring semester. One year later we stood together on African soil, young full-time missionaries with hearts afire for the nations of the world. Nearly three decades and fifty-some countries later the fire still burns. And thanks to what I learned from these priceless

brothers, I still stand. Thank you both for the invitation to
Room A.

I met Steve and Annette Melendez when I took my dead
laptop to their computer store in Kahului, Hawaii. Their
timely work, compassionate rates, and constant praise to God
were the serendipity that enabled me to navigate the modern
writer's nightmare with only minor dings to my psyche. It was
worth it to gain such friends.

Finally, deepest thanks to my new friends at Bethany
House Publishers for your trust and patience, and for the cof-
fee last Christmas. You didn't have to do it. But since you did
. . . I drink decaf.

Contents

God Is God:
So You Don't Have to Be

"I'm not into religion," my driver informed me as I loaded my suitcases into the trunk of his car. Kenny was an off-duty Washington, D.C., cop, whose mom had assigned him the task of transporting me from Dulles International Airport, outside the city, to Front Royal, Virginia, an hour away. I knew the routine because I had been through it several times before.

It's something like this:

Jane (the praying mom/wife) is a devoted Christian who loves John (her irreligious son/husband) and wants to see him give his life to Christ. But Jane can't bring up religion around John; he doesn't want to hear it. Then she finds out that I, the straight-shooting, guest-speaking missionary, am coming to town. Inspiration hits: Maybe spending an hour in the relaxed surroundings of a car with someone who "witnesses professionally" (me) will do it! She volunteers to take care of my ride from the airport, letting me in on the plan. "He won't listen to any of us, Jim. But you have such a way with words. Maybe you can get through."

Kenny was not dumb. As he made his way to the airport, he was already steeling himself. In his mind he was about to face a dreaded "right-wing, Bible-pounding preacher."

I climbed into the car feeling all the stiffness of this very uncomfortable setting. We weren't even past the last parked taxi when Kenny repeated, "Nope, I'm not into religion. I'm an atheist."

"I doubt it," I said, chuckling. That was all.

Kenny looked shocked, and before he could recover I added, "Hey, how are the Orioles doing? Wish I could get to a game. I grew up in Baltimore, when Brooks was at third and Belanger played shortstop."

"Uh, I don't know. . . . Whaddaya mean, you doubt it?"

"Oh, I've never met a real atheist," I replied. "Not even in all the communist countries where I traveled for years. So far, in my experience, they've all turned out to be just very frightened believers." Then I switched gears. "You know, when I was a kid my cousin and I would take the city bus all the way across town to the Orioles games. It was a lot safer back then."

"Well, maybe I should call myself an agnostic," Kenny said, ignoring baseball altogether.

"Naw, I doubt that too," I answered with a wave, and reinvoked America's pastime.

Back and forth we went for another ten minutes, me tossing baseballs, and Kenny striking out at faith in God. Finally he became frustrated with not being able to find a polite way to prove just how ungodly he was.

"Why don't you believe me?" he asked with a tone that said he no longer believed himself either.

I zeroed in—not for the kill, but to wound him just enough for the marksman God would send into his life after me. "Look, I'm trying to talk about baseball. You're the one who keeps changing the subject back to religion. A real atheist or agnostic wouldn't care as much as you obviously do!"

We both laughed, and this time Kenny nodded in half-surrender. I could have bored in on him after that, but I didn't. For the next forty-five minutes we talked a little more about God, baseball, and police work, but we mainly just enjoyed the ride together toward the Blue Ridge Mountains. Then he dropped me off in Front Royal and was gone.

So why didn't I try to lead him to Christ? Why didn't I at least ask him if I could "have a word of prayer" with him? Because, in my experience, that wasn't what Kenny needed. It wasn't my role in his life. God had given me what, in the movies, they call a "walk-on" part in His plan for Kenny. All He wanted from me, all He *required* of me, was that I enable this young bachelor to relax around a Christian man for about an hour, and then drive away not feeling assaulted, or worse, emasculated.

By the way, God did bring someone after me. Kenny's mom's assistant pastor invited the young policeman to church. He tried to wangle out of it, of course, by saying he'd attend a service only if the clergyman would agree to ride in the squad car with him through the mean streets of downtown Washington. But to his shock the pastor agreed, and Kenny soon found himself spending hour after hour discussing God in surroundings dangerous enough to make an otherwise tough man bare his soul.

Six months later, when I returned to northern Virginia for another speaking engagement, I saw him again, this time heading at me full speed, grinning. Kenny could hardly wait to tell me that he had committed his life to Jesus Christ, and was no longer the frightened believer I had met outside Dulles Airport.

Who's the Savior Here, Anyway?

"But what if he had wrecked his car and died ten minutes after you said goodbye?" That's the kind of question that Christians sometimes ask each other—and it transforms a proper sense that it's important to share our faith into the threat of blame if we don't take every opportunity to "close the sale" in leading people to Christ. Most of us aren't great salesmen, of course, so we struggle through life, blanketed by ever-deepening layers of guilt. And the pile gets a little higher every time we hear an evangelist tell another car-wreck story.

If you're one of those guys nagged by the constant "what-if" threat, then I'm about to tell you the most liberating news since your driving instructor said you passed. Here it is: God is God so you don't have to be! "God so loved the world," which only He is big enough to do. You only have to love *your* world, which probably consists of fewer people than you think. What's more, God loves the people in your world more than you do. And His ways of bringing them to faith are not limited by your cowardice or lack of communication skills. He isn't helpless if you let Him down. He is still God.

God doesn't necessarily want you to turn every gas stop, elevator ride, and mealtime into a soul-winning safari. There's a time to speak up and a time to shut up, to just eat your lunch without feeling guilty. You don't have to turn every conversation into a conversion.

You and I are just the salt of the earth, not the Savior of the world. The Holy Spirit guides us into being like Jesus. Guilt pushes us, not to be *like* the Savior but to actually try to *be* the savior sometimes.

Guilt is a terrible taskmaster. I used to think I was worth nothing more to God than my next trip to Russia. I'd hear other missionaries talk about God providing free stadium rent for their crusades and how the prime minister's wife got healed the first night and then the whole army wanted Bibles and . . . It made me feel worthless, guilt-ridden. No matter how hard I worked, God probably never would be satisfied with my "output."

Back home in Baltimore I was everybody's favorite—the pastor's son who became a missionary to the world's danger zones. I had a ton of great tales, some of which you'll read in this book. And when I came home to tell them, the congregation would give me the closest thing to a ticker-tape parade that a seventy-five-member church could give. My stories had added punch because I was young, committed, and best of all, broke. (Being broke always makes missions stories more effective. The only thing better is being dead, and having someone else tell them for you.) The people would *ooh* and *ahh* and then say things like, "Boy, it must be so exciting to actually be out there on the front lines doing something for God!" And I would nod and say *yes*, it was, because it was. It was great being on the front lines. But that wasn't the problem.

Coming home was the problem. I still didn't feel as though I had done enough, like I was worth anything. I would tell the stories and then go back to my room still hollow inside, feeling like I didn't even know God very well. In fact, I felt the way a discouraged pastor described it to me years later in Oklahoma: "Sometimes it seems as though I know everything about Christianity except Christ."

Actually, as I look back on it, that was pretty accurate. After all, I stayed so busy working for God that I hardly ever took time just to enjoy Him. I traveled for Him, sang for Him, preached for Him, and showed countless people in foreign countries how to pray their first prayer to Him. But I didn't have time to *enjoy* Him. I was just too busy, and besides, the prospect intimidated me to death.

It wasn't that I doubted my need to spend more time praying and reading the Bible—preferably before 6:30 A.M., of course, if I was really serious. On the contrary, I was thoroughly convinced of the importance of "devotions." I had been ever since being informed of it by a fellow five-year-old in Sunday school back in Mud Fork, West Virginia. But I've also needed flu shots and enemas from time to time, and never once have I gotten excited at the prospect of either.

Auld Angst Signs

Guilt for not praying and studying the Bible is only one of the spooks haunting the hallways of Christian men's minds. This unfriendly ghost has cousins—co-conspirators that work to keep you quiet and defeated. Every time the prospect of giv-

ing voice to your faith in Christ presents itself, the ghosts of
Failure, Inadequacy, and Hypocrisy flit past your ear, whispering the lines that have worked so well ever since Saint Peter chickened out by a campfire near Calvary.

The ghost of *Failure* leads off with a whisper, dredging up
memories of the few attempts you made right after you became
a Christian.

- You got completely tongued-tied.
- He brought up questions you couldn't answer.
- She got mad and has avoided you ever since.
- They laughed at you and called you a Jesus Freak.
- You hated knocking on doors.

The sound of forty pounds of wood slamming in your face
is still fresh in your mind, when *Inadequacy* steps up to tell
you you're just not cut out for this, pointing out very good reasons for you to keep quiet.

- You're not a good speaker.
- You're not smart enough to debate.
- You don't even understand the Bible yourself.
- You're the last person your dad (cousin, brother) would
  listen to.
- You can't take confrontation.

Finally, *Hypocrisy* chimes in, irritated with you for even
bringing up such a ridiculous idea, in light of your obvious
lack of ability and clear record of failure. His tone is outright
accusatory. Why pretend?

- You still wrestle with your own doubts.
- You have enough trouble with your own dirty mind.
- You don't even like the little nerd.
- Your brothers have seen you at your worst; they know all
  your faults.
- You've lived next door for twelve years and never once
  mentioned God. What gives you the right to start now?

- He's effeminate and makes your skin crawl.
- The things that cross your mind when you look at her . . . it would be so hypocritical.

As quickly as it came to you, the idea of sharing your Christian faith makes tracks for the pit of your stomach, where it will remain suppressed until you meet someone else who needs the God you know. Then you'll rehearse the same little episode again, feeling ever more the failure, as *Guilt* pedals through the cycle faster each time.

It would be nice to say these lines are all just devilish lies. But most of them are probably true, which is why they're so effective. *The Enemy of our souls is not opposed to the truth if he can make it do the work of a lie. But the truth about us is not the ultimate problem. The problem is the lie* that Satan sneaks in with those ugly but accurate observations about you. Like the prize in a box of Cracker Jack℠, it's hidden in every one. Here it is—

You'll never change. God wants you to, but you can't.

Most of us swallow this one whole, accepting it as an immutable fact on the grounds that we know ourselves better than anyone else. But we're wrong. God knows you and me better than we know ourselves. And He will change us as we spend time in His Word, in prayer—and spend time just plain liking and caring about people.

Guilt about ourselves and our failures is something we *can* resolve handily with a God who loves us—a Father who wants us to come running home from all our prodigal pigsties for a good soul bath. And to hear, "I forgive you, son." That is offered *freely*.

Willingness and feeling *prepared* to tell someone about our faith in God is another matter. And under it all lies this big hurdle: the *hello-do-you-know-Jesus* kind of witnessing feels like an *unnatural act* for most men. We instinctively see it as an act of aggression, and therefore something to avoid. Television's Jay Leno once described a group of Christians who knocked on his door to ask him if he knew Jesus. "For a minute," he mugged, "I was afraid they were going to try and gang-save me!" It's a crude joke, but it sheds light on the way well-meaning Christians often are perceived. If Mother Teresa held a gun on you, your feelings would be mainly in reaction to the gun, not the nun.

As for me, I'd rather go golfing. *Tee-to-green* is better than *door-to-door* on any day of my year. Besides, the golf course is probably a better place to share your faith than ten inches away from someone's screen door, which is an owner-installed device to keep pests out. Out on the fairway the scenery is gorgeous, and the footing is equal.

Okay, the middle of a golf game may or may not be ideal. (You don't want to ruin your partner's putting while saving his soul.) But the point remains: it is a great first step if you're not comfortable going up on a stranger's porch. And more natural, which means you're more likely to say what you really want to say in the way you want to say it. Indeed, God has given us a brilliant "pre-qualifying" device, especially for winning people to Christ. It's called *friendship*. Jesus even gave us the strategy for employing this incredible witnessing tool. He said, "You shall love your neighbor as yourself." What a concept! How utterly different from the "I might be a Christian or I might be the IRS" front-door invasive approach.

Roy Rogers vs. Mr. Rogers

That isn't to say that nobody ever became a Christian at the hands of a door-knocking stranger. But face it, there's a reason why there just aren't that many Christians in a race with the Avon Lady: it's unnatural and, for most men, very unpleasant. Do *you* like it when an uninvited stranger walks up to the border of your private world and starts asking highly personal questions? No. Nobody does. So why would you want to *be* that stranger, doing unto others what you would *not* want done to you?

The porch soldiers, they're wonderful folks, but they're a special breed. They're the General George Pattons of God's army. You're Dick van Patten. They're Crocodile Dundee. You're Captain Kangaroo. They're Roy Rogers. You're Mister Rogers.

That's God's army, you think, and you don't fit in anywhere. The General Pattons have *finished* their prayers and other spiritual calisthenics by 6:00 in the morning . . . while you're groping for that annoying alarm clock.

Which brings us back to the big lie: You'll never change— you *can't* change. But in truth you can.

The first step is to stop making comparisons between yourself and those Christians who are "just a lot better at it." If someone has "the gift" of being a walking witnessing machine, remember it *is* a "gift" and not the rule.

We were not necessarily meant to measure up to each other: We are offered the chance to come to God and let Him change us and cause us to stand up for Him. In the way *He* chooses. With the people *He* brings into our lives. Why be concerned that you're not "brave" enough to go out and knock on the doors of strangers, or preach on street corners, when there are plenty of opportunities to stand up for Christ in your own little world?

That brings up another matter of concern. Your own world, and the various people in it. Most of us men take a look around and realize our lives are filled with *the* oddest assortment of people. Dirty-jokers. New Agers. Politically correct sophisticates who are placidly, irritatingly "tolerant" of everyone— except *Christians.* Your world is peopled with skeptics, cynics, agnostics and so-called atheists. Not to mention members of your family, and old friends, who present perhaps the biggest challenges when it comes to talking freely about your faith.

Everywhere you turn, I'll bet you find mostly people who are just *itching* to have you speak up for Christ. So they can blast your words out of the air, that is, and help you realize that (a) your beliefs are wrong, or (b) your witness is as welcome as a burp at the Queen's tea party. You can sense it, can't you—the eagerness for you to speak so they can target-practice on the syllables as they launch from your lips.

Why would you want to stand up, and speak up, for Christ before this firing squad?

In fact, I want to help you see that there are very simple, practical ways to talk about your faith with all these characters in your life. And actually come away without too many bulletholes in your soul. So we'll take a look together at how to address each one of these groups.

Beyond the Guilt and Snipers

But perhaps the biggest reason we men don't speak up about our faith is that we really don't feel prepared to. Men *hate* to feel shoved-out-there, on the front line, where we might be shown up as less than adequate. It's not the greatest male trait, and we'll look at it a little more closely later.

Essentially, you do need to be prepared to talk about Christ—and be armed with more than a few tracts and secondhand opinions. The people in your life will have probing questions, you're *right*! And you don't need seminary training, but you do need to know what's so good about the "good news" of the Gospel. And you can find tremendous encouragement and motivation—not *guilt*—in understanding the greatness of Jesus' "Great Commission" that sends us obediently out to stand for Him before an unbelieving and searching world. Your world.

As we dive in together, I want more than anything to encourage you with this. You can close your eyes and imagine the face of anyone you want—from the foulest to the fairest—and rest in the sure knowledge that God is *already* at work in their life and heart. Oh, it may be well concealed behind obvious sins, indifference, or self-satisfied complacency, but He *is* at work!

That is to remind you, God *is* God, so you don't have to be. And He said He will be right there with us, giving us special encouragement as we learn how to boldly speak for the honor of His name.

And what we need to do is follow His lead.

Believing He has gone ahead of us, in the hearts of people we know, let's go.

For Thought and Discussion

1. Has anyone ever used guilt or pressure to make you feel that you're a dismal example of a Christian unless you are speaking up for Christ all the time, in every situation? What is the effect of guilty pressure on any undertaking that is placed on us?
2. Take stock of some of the people in your world—at work, in the community, among your friends. What spoken or un-spoken "resistances" would face you if you tried to speak up about your faith in Christ?
3. Maybe you're a new Christian, or a man who's experiencing a renewal of faith. What can you do to prepare yourself to witness for Christ?

The Greatness of the Great Commission

Picture yourself by a campfire on a mountain in Galilee. . . .

There He stood, the same man whose lifeless body they had laid to rest only a few evenings earlier. At least His general appearance was right. And there was that unmistakable smile—more in the eyes than on the mouth. But His clothes were new, and too clean to have made the journey up this mountain.

The men smiled back, in fearful compliance more than joy. Only Peter drew closer. Scars above the man's eyes were still pink. It *was* Jesus! There was the bare patch on His jaw, where a soldier had pulled out His beard. If He had overcome death, why were the marks—any marks—still there? The disciple wondered if the pain of the last week might be more than a memory too.

The sound of his own name dissolved Peter's reverie, and with it everyone's doubts. Jesus was greeting each of the eleven, and each man, as if on cue, began either to laugh or to weep at the sound of the Savior speaking his name. Soon all of them were kneeling, worshiping at His feet.

Minutes became hours, and afternoon turned to evening. The laughter and tears continued, the latter gradually evaporating into worn-out relief. Andrew built a fire. The glow and crackle invoked quiet conversation and meditative stares, the kind that inevitably form questions. Would Jesus go to Jerusalem? What would He do to the Jews and Romans? Had He seen His mother? Had He known about Judas from the start? Why were they meeting in Galilee? One query led to five, and five to fifty. Jesus answered most of them, laughing occasionally, dismissing a few with a gentle wave.

Then John asked about the "new covenant" Jesus had described during the previous week's Passover supper. That would prove to be the final question of the evening, as Jesus leaned forward and, beginning with Moses, explained to them late into the night how all the covenants of Scripture had anticipated this one.

Jesus took His men to all the mountains where the holy covenants had been made, mountains where the decrees of God had been given.

Past the fire and through the trees Peter could see the softly lit villages of Galilee in the valleys below, where Jew and Gentile lives mingled like the lights of their candles. Samaria's northern neighbors had no idea what was happening in the hills above them, no idea that the resurrected Messiah was so close by. If only they could hear what Jesus was saying, the mysteries of the ages He was explaining, right here on this . . . this mountain!

Peter's eyes darted from the fire to the face of Jesus, who stopped mid-sentence and smiled—no, grinned at him. The Savior's eyes seemed to blaze even more brightly than the campfire they reflected. The fisherman was finally beginning to understand.

The Lord of all the earth was about to proclaim the terms of a New Covenant for the nations. What better place than a mountain in "Galilee of the Gentiles," right where the nations mingled with the people of God!

Jesus spoke again. His tone was different now, like that of a monarch attending to the affairs of a newly conquered kingdom.

"All authority in heaven and on earth has been given to me. Therefore go and make disciples of all nations, baptizing them in the name of the Father and of the Son and of the Holy Spirit, and teaching them to obey everything I have commanded you. And surely I will be with you always, to the very end of the age" (Matthew 28:18–20).

Then there was stillness, as though time had indeed stopped, and was awaiting His next command. Only the dancing flame and the cricket chorus in the night air kept the world going.

The men were mute, not stricken by fear but by the awesome moment. A tax collector, a physician, some fishermen, and a few other nondescripts had ascended this mountain not many hours ago. Now they were world-changers, the apostles of Jesus Christ.

The Savior watched with serene satisfaction the transformation sparked by His brief orders. He would speak no more this night, and would shortly leave in the same way He had come. He looked at His champions one last time, His very gaze delivering the command to each by name.

Go, Peter. Go, Andrew, John, and James. Baptize them, Philip, Nathanael, Matthew, and Thaddaeus. Teach them, James, Simon, and Thomas. And remember, I am with you to the end. You can do the job. Now, go. . . .

———

Remember when Nissan was Datsun? The company's slogan back then was "We a-a-are . . . driven!" With the way I used to understand the Great Commission, I was driven, too. Driven to tell my fifth-grade teacher, Mr. Setzer, that I'd have to sit out the class square-dance lesson, because "my religion doesn't allow it." Driven to take a lonely stand in a high-school sociology discussion on whether "Man is born basically good," or "Man is essentially selfish and hedonistic." (I won that one, even though I wasn't sure what "hedonistic" meant.)

I was driven to drop a full college scholarship, become a missionary at eighteen, and head off to South Africa with a dozen other equally driven young Christians.

Twenty-seven years and sixty countries later I'm still driven. But what's under my hood, what powers me upward and onward, has changed even more than the motor in a Z-car.

You see, I'm not a "Type-A personality," the proverbial heart attack in a business suit. I've never wanted to build a big ministry outreach, or go on television, or even be known as an evangelist. (I don't even use hair spray.) I've always preferred to keep our world headquarters in a downstairs bedroom, avoid inspiration that would get me into debt, and to restrict our mailing list to the names of people I've actually met.

That's not to say there aren't some admirable Type-A's around. I've waltzed through quite a few open doors that got that way because one of these guys bulldozed it. And they undoubtedly sign more payroll checks than anybody else in God's gallery of dispositions. We should be thankful for them. Type-A's are able to turn the Great Commission into a franchise operation. But I'm not one of them, and really don't want to be!

So what motivates an alphabetically challenged man like me to log more than three million miles, sharing the Gospel everywhere from Shea Stadium to secret Russian prayer meetings?

True, I started out enthused, pumped—pure adrenaline with sideburns and a Bible! But then, in South Africa, and later in places like Trinidad, Poland, and Vietnam, I saw the "teeming masses" I had always heard about. They really *were* poor and hungry. Even on a teenage missionary's meager budget I had so much more than they did.

Twenty dollars that came in the Christmas mail in Hong Kong quickly became ten, as I gave half away. There were so many poor people, I *had* to help somebody.

But before long my enthusiasm for the Good News had been replaced by *guilt* and *pity*. No matter how much I gave, no matter how diligently I served God, it never seemed to be enough. There were always more needs than I could meet, maybe more than anyone could meet.

Have you ever been moved by a sermon about barefooted, starving children in Africa, only to wind up feeling blamed because you owned extra pairs of shoes or didn't finish your cold mashed potatoes? That's *guilt* and *pity* at work. It's why missions conferences don't outdraw football games.

How about those alarming government statistics that blame crime rates on hunger and poverty, as a set-up for raising middle-class taxes? That's *guilt* and *pity* at work in politics.

Guilt and *pity* are terrible motivators. They distort the Gospel, or even worse, completely silence it, as we discussed in Chapter 1. Self-condemnation aborts ministry before it can be born.

I was also plagued by a *good news/bad news* complex:

- The good news is that Jesus Christ came to save the world.
- The bad new is that it's too far gone to save. But you are obligated to pull hard against a riptide of darkness and apathy.

Let me ask you a question: What are we presenting to people? Is the purpose of witnessing (a) to kill yourself to rescue a few souls in a world that, for the most part, doesn't care, or (b) to proclaim that the nations belong to Jesus Christ, a Savior who looks upon men with compassion, and is ready to deliver them into His Father's care?

Which of those choices would you call good news? If you said "b," congratulations! You're in agreement with the writers of both Testaments, the great theologians of history, plus the founding fathers of America and most of Western civilization. But if you said "a," well, no wonder you hesitate to tell anyone you're a Christian!

It took me fourteen years of missionary frustration to discover the good news, fourteen years before I finally discovered the "greatness" of the Great Commission.

Let me tell you what made the difference.

Great Expectations

After His resurrection, Jesus called eleven ordinary, somewhat undependable men to an obscure mountain in Galilee. He proceeded to give them the biggest job assignment in the history of the world. Long ago our Christian forefathers dubbed it the Great Commission. And no wonder! The Savior's expectations were extraordinary, and to Jewish sensibilities, revolutionary.

The only covenant these men knew had always pointed them to Jerusalem. Now Jesus was calling them away from that city, bringing them instead to the very area He previously had ordered them to avoid!

These twelve Jesus sent out with the following instructions: "Do not go among the Gentiles or enter any town of the Samaritans. Go rather to the lost sheep of Israel. As you go, preach this message: 'The kingdom of heaven is near' " (Matthew 10:5–6).

Israel. God had called His people out from the world into this *nation.* It was the apple of His eye, the place where He dwelt. But now, with His "new" covenant, Jesus was sending them *from* Israel *into* the world, armed with the Gospel—the Good News of the kingdom of God!

At last they began to see clearly. Jesus' life, His ministry, His crucifixion and resurrection, even the salvation of the Gentiles—these had been Jehovah's intention all along, and the Savior had known it! They had even heard Him quote the psalmist, but had been too dull to understand at the time.

The stone the builders rejected has become the capstone; the LORD has done this, and it is marvelous in our eyes (Psalm 118:22–23, cf. Matthew 21:42).

Brilliance, sheer brilliance. The apostle Paul would later call it "God's secret wisdom, a wisdom that has been hidden and that God destined for our glory before time began. None of the rulers of this age understood it, for if they had, they would not have crucified the Lord of glory" (1 Corinthians 2:7–8).

Satan and his followers had been blindsided, the serpent's head crushed from above. Only as the blow struck was the divine mockery made plain to him. The soldiers were driving the wooden cross, with Jesus on it, into the soil that formed the crown of Golgotha. Even as life was ebbing from His helpless frame, the blood of atonement trickled from Jesus' wounded heel to the earth beneath Him, shattering the serpent's skull! God had kept a promise made in the garden. The enemy would never recover.

It was this wonderful irony that the ascended Savior celebrated when, "having disarmed the powers and authorities, he made a public spectacle of them, triumphing over them by the cross" (Colossians 2:15).

And it was the sweetness of having beaten the world's greatest con artist at his own game that Jesus tasted on that mountain in Galilee. No wonder His expectation of victory was so complete, so unwavering, as He uttered His preposterous proposition: that eleven heretofore unreliable men should go and change the world in His name!

Maybe we ought to take another look at what He said that day. What turned these weaklings into such doctrinal giants, spiritual architects who changed the world within their own generation?

Here are the words of Jesus:

All authority in heaven and on earth has been given to me. Therefore go and make disciples of all nations, baptizing them in the name of the Father and of the Son and

of the Holy Spirit, and teaching them to obey everything I have commanded you. And surely I will be with
you always, to the very end of the age (Matthew 28:18–
20).

There is an obvious pattern here. Jesus keeps repeating one
word, emphasizing one idea several times. He has *all* authority. His New Covenant involves *all* nations. *All* new disciples
are to be baptized. They are to be taught *all* of His commandments. He will be with those whom He is commissioning *always*, that is, until the job is finished. Jesus is consumed with
certainty, confident in the extreme. And it sounds as though
He wants His listeners (and Matthew's readers) to go over-
board too. Let's examine each "all," and I think you'll see why
this magnificent obsession changed my life . . . and gave me
enough fire to talk to anyone about it.

All Authority

First Jesus said, "All authority in heaven and on earth has
been given to me." It may surprise you to learn that, in the
original Greek manuscript, this word "all" actually meant
ALL! There is no neutral territory, no place up in space or here
below, where He is not Lord of all, nothing that He does not
call *mine*.

But do we really believe this? Or have we fallen for what
someone has called the "myth of neutrality," the mistaken belief that there are some places where Jesus is not Lord?

- Some educators believe that He may be Lord elsewhere,
  but not in *their* classrooms. There not even His name is
  appropriate for discussion, much less His commandments.
- Some politicians believe that it is wise to be seen in God's
  house on Sundays, especially as election day approaches,
  but that lordship has its limits. After all, they opine, you
  can't mix religion and politics. You can't legislate moral-
  ity. Don't forget about the separation of church and state.

After all, we're a pluralistic society!

- Some doctors, lawyers, and businessmen say that He may well be Lord, but He has nothing to say about their professions or the way they run their offices. The Bible doesn't speak to today's situations, they claim. Or maybe Scripture applies at church, but this is business. I'm an equal opportunity employer; I have to remain neutral.

Christians should have no doubt. When Jesus Christ claimed to have been given "all authority . . . in heaven and on earth," He was rightfully proclaiming himself to be the head of every state, chief justice of every court, headmaster of every school, chairman of every board, pastor of every church, head of every household, owner of all the cattle *and* the hills, and heir of all the earth. From Boston to Beijing, sandlot to stadium, post office to Oval Office, Jesus Christ is Lord of ALL!

All Nations

Matthew 28:19 contains one of the most famous phrases in the Bible, as well as one of the most misinterpreted and misunderstood. "Therefore go and make disciples of all the nations. . . ." Oh, we know what that means. We're supposed to make sure that every nation hears the Gospel. But is that what Jesus is saying here? No.

We should expect that at least *some* people will be saved in every country on earth, then, right? No, He isn't saying that either.

The Interlinear New Testament in Greek & English[1] renders Jesus' words shorter, sweeter, and more to the point: "Going, therefore, disciple ye all the nations." *That* is what He said! It may seem like Mission Impossible, but it is what the Savior said. We are not merely to inform; we don't just make converts. Our orders are to disciple all the nations (Greek: *ethnos*, meaning "peoples").

This means that we can expect Christ's Gospel to produce

widespread results. It means we can expect entire cities to repent and be transformed, just as Nineveh did and was. It
means we're not fools for dreaming those outrageous dreams
of seeing whole societies come to Jesus, or of hearing a president lead a nation in a prayer of repentance. It means missionaries can take the Gospel across the seas, with full confidence that it was designed to succeed!

> In the same way, let your light shine before men, that
> they may see your good deeds and praise your Father
> in heaven (Matthew 5:16).

Theologians can debate the end times, and prophecy buffs
can play pin-the-tail-on-the-Antichrist into the Third Millen-
nium. But nobody can deny, in light of what Jesus commanded
in this verse, that we Christians have lately set our sights too
low. The One with *all* authority clearly has His eye on *all*
nations, no doubt due to a promise His Father made in Psalm
110, the Old Testament chapter quoted more often in the New
Testament than any other:

> The LORD said to my LORD: "Sit at my right hand until
> I make your enemies a footstool for your feet." The
> LORD will extend your mighty scepter from Zion; you
> will rule in the midst of your enemies (Psalm 110:1–2).

No wonder He has such great expectations! Jesus rules *in
the midst* of His enemies. He rules NOW! That's why He can
give the order to disciple *all* nations.

All Baptized

Just when He had them boggled at the notion of "all
nations," Jesus added the words, "baptizing them in the name
of the Father and of the Son and of the Holy Spirit." He wasn't
offering this as an optional ceremony; He wanted it done.
Why?

Someone said God's favorite way to destroy a sinner is to save him. That's what baptism symbolizes: destruction and salvation, death, burial, and resurrection. Baptism represents inclusion in the New Covenant and membership in Christ's Church, just as circumcision did in the Old Covenant. Jesus said He would build His Church, and evidently He envisioned quite a large construction project.

But how do you baptize nations? The answer is no joke. You do it . . . one person at a time.

That wouldn't be so intimidating if we were just talking the Falkland Islands, or some little tribe in the Peruvian jungle. But Russia, India, China . . . Las Vegas? Hey, this *is* Mission Impossible. ("Good morning, Mr. Phelps. Your mission, should you decide to accept . . . naah, forget it! Your brain will self-destruct in five seconds.")

There's a simple reason why our minds tilt at such a prospect: The world is too big and we're too small. After all, we haven't conquered Satan, like Jesus, or been raised from the dead, like Jesus, or been seated at the right hand of the Father, like Jesus, or . . . Hey, wait a minute . . . we have!

> But because of his great love for us, God, who is rich in mercy, made us alive with Christ even when we were dead in transgressions—it is by grace you have been saved. And God raised us up with Christ and seated us with him in the heavenly realms in Christ Jesus (Ephesians 2:4–6).

> I write to you, fathers, because you have known him who is from the beginning. I write to you, young men, because you are strong, and the word of God lives in you, and you have overcome the evil one (1 John 2:14).

God has adopted us to be His sons, like Jesus (Galatians 4:5), given us His Holy Spirit, like Jesus (4:6), and made us His legitimate heirs, like Jesus (4:7). Why has He done all of this? So that we will learn how to think and act *just like Jesus*. And Jesus isn't worried or intimidated in the least when faced with the job of baptizing nations. Remember, He has all authority and rules in the midst of His enemies. He knows that *"nothing is impossible with God"* (Luke 1:37, emphasis added).

All Commandments

"Teaching them to obey everything I have commanded you."

In a way, we've been given the mind of Jesus in the form of the Bible's sixty-six books. Unfortunately, the notion has become pretty common that only the last twenty-seven actually count, that the New Testament somehow replaced the Old Testament. So let's get our terms straight: The New *Covenant* replaced the old one, but the New *Testament* was *added* to the Old. Concerning the Bible, we can say that the testaments are records giving witness to the covenants. Since the Old Testament gives witness to both the Old and New Covenants, we still respect its authority, as modified—not negated—by the New Testament.

Still the error persists. People treat the first thirty-nine books of Scripture as though they were God's first draft, but with too much sex and violence and too many rules. They prefer the "kinder and gentler" New Testament. Once a man told me that he couldn't even remember the last time he had read the Old Testament, since "none of it matters anymore anyway." That man was a pastor.

Of course the apostle Paul read it, as did Matthew, Mark, Luke, John, Peter, Jude, and whoever wrote Hebrews. The Old Testament was the only Bible they had. It was where they discovered most of what they learned about Jesus. In fact, this was the Bible Jesus used to preach about himself.

He said to them, "This is what I told you while I was still with you: Everything must be fulfilled that is written about me in the Law of Moses, the Prophets and the Psalms." Then he opened their minds so they could understand the Scriptures (Luke 24:44–45).

There it is: it's all about Him! From Moses' first "Thou shalt" to David's final "Praise the Lord," the Bible is about Jesus. That's why we're supposed to teach it—all of it—when making disciples. The more they know of it, the more they'll follow Him.

Here are three very important statements to remember:

- God's Word reveals Jesus, because Jesus *is* God's Word in the flesh.
- God's rule includes God's rules. The whole Bible is still the Bible.
- You can't teach others something you, yourself, don't know.

Oh, why did I put that last one in there? Now I've heaped all the guilt back on you. . . . Not really, here's your relief: Remember, the Great Commission is a group project. You can't teach everybody everything, because you can't learn it all yourself. Only Jesus knows *all* His commandments.

Just do your part. Treasure what you *do* know; rejoice in it, and ask God to teach you more. Get together with friends and dive into those tough parts—even Leviticus, the literary sleeping pill of men everywhere! Remember, even the laws that seem archaic and harsh to us, King David called "more precious than gold" (Psalm 19:10). The apostle Paul told Timothy that "the law is good if one uses it properly" (1 Timothy 1:8). In other words, use God's law properly, and not legalistically.

Then, when the joy in your heart starts losing ground to the whirring in your brain, thank God you don't have to know everything!

Always

Jesus knew He was blowing circuits in blue-collar minds when He told the disciples to do "all" these incredible deeds.

He knew they would be intimidated and overwhelmed, just like you might be right now. So He added a fifth and final "all," one that would permanently remove any misgivings they might be suffering. He said, "And surely I am with you *always*, to the very end of the age."

Imagine your dad picking you up to throw you into the deep end of the pool, and then promising to personally stay with you, teach you, and protect you until you learn to swim. It's like Jesus saying, "I, the one with all authority in heaven and on earth, will stay with you until that which I've commanded you is fulfilled."

The disciples weren't reading this in a book, or simply feeling assured of it in their hearts. *He* was standing right there in front of them. Last week He was dead, and now He was *with* them! And He was promising to remain with them "to the very end of the age." This "Immanuel," whose birth had been announced in Matthew's first chapter, was declaring himself to be God-with-us on a permanent basis.

Almost two thousand years have passed since they heard those words. Their work continues.

The Greatness of Your Commission

Of course, it doesn't matter how convinced you are that the Gospel is good news, if you can't express it to someone else in clear, easy-to-understand terms. Or if you mention something wonderful like God's creation, only to be shot down by some Charles Darwin wannabe who challenges you to explain dinosaur bones in Iowa.

What do you say? How much do you have to know? When do you shut up? Can I go home now?

One of my favorite aspects of the Good News is that I don't have to save the world. Only Jesus can do that. I just have to be flat-footed, golf-loving, word-processing me.

I also don't have to turn you into me. After all, Jesus has

commissioned you to be *you*, whether you're a Type-A achievement junkie or Gomer Pyle's assistant at the Mayberry gas station.

What I do want to show you is how to be the *you* God made *in front of other people.* (Of course if you're a slob with mustard on your shirt, don't take that too literally.) We all need improving. We all need to know the Bible better, to pray more. . . .

But we don't all have to be the world's greatest theologians, armed with unanswerable brilliance in the face of every question. Nor do we have to be Perry Mason defending God. No, we just have to be witnesses to *the facts we know.* And nothing more.

So relax, and read on.

For Thought and Discussion

1. What difference does it make knowing that *all* authority has been given to Christ, as you tell other people about your faith in Him?
2. What is the "world" God has "commissioned" you to reach? Who lives in it? How do you relate to them now?
3. If you are feeling driven by guilt to share the Gospel, and not because you are enthusiastically grateful for what God has done in your life—how will you get rid of that guilt? Remember, guilt and fear are poor motivators!
4. Rather than getting overwhelmed by the thought of "all those people" you know who need to hear the Gospel, pray and ask God to open your eyes to the simple, daily opportunities to speak of your trust in Him.

Notes

1. Alfred Marshall, *The Interlinear KJV-NIV Parallel New Testament in Greek & English* (Grand Rapids: Zondervan, 1991).

Preparing to Take a Stand

The God of peace will soon crush Satan under your feet (Romans 16:20).

The Indonesian translator was already intimidated when our fair-skinned trombonist stepped to the microphone. Besides not being a believer, the interpreter had learned English from books and wasn't used to hearing it. While Tom, the budding young preacher, spoke an American vernacular that broke all the rules his interpreter was struggling to remember. The sermon quickly became a game of linguistic bumper cars.

"That if thou shalt confess with thy mouth the Lord Jesus, and shalt believe in thine heart . . ." quoted Tom. It might as well have been Pig Latin. Both men were bewildered—the translator by this Shakespearean description of being born a second time, and the American by his own inability to express himself.

It was a long night, but for Tom it proved to be a stepping-stone on the road to becoming a fine preacher. (For the Indonesians it was, well . . . a long night.)

What would you have done in Tom's place? Could you have explained Romans 10:9 in simple terms? Could you describe "sin" to a Chinese audience whose language doesn't include a word for *sin*? (Or a Western audience, for that matter.) Could you explain the biblical concept of "final judgment" in terms of linear time to an Indian audience that believes in spiraling time and reincarnation?

Here's a real toughie: If asked, could you tell the guy next door how to commit his life to Christ and be born again? "Might as well bring on the Indonesians," you say. "I just wouldn't know the right words. But God would bring someone else along. Right?"

But the Lord has chosen *you* to live next door to the man next door, hasn't He? He has placed you there for His purposes. You might not feel up to the task but, frankly, you're not the first.

No good at public speaking, even one on one? Moses was a stutterer.

Don't have a commanding presence? The apostle Paul is reputed to have been a squinty little guy with bad eyesight and perhaps other, more severe, handicaps.

Ashamed of your past? Matthew was a tax collector: Imagine Ebenezer Scrooge working for the Roman IRS.

Then there was Solomon, the adulterer—and his father, David, a murderer *and* an adulterer.

Of course, among them, these five wholly inadequate men also successfully challenged Pharaoh, killed a giant, preached to Caesar, and wrote twenty of the Bible's sixty-six books. Now what was that about not being qualified?

Look, you know by now that you don't have to turn into one of those walking witnessing machines we marveled at in Chapter 1. But wouldn't you like to be able to explain your faith to people without them wondering if you're an alien lifeform? Or to have the confidence to speak up intelligently when some local antichrist is barbecuing "right-wing Christians" at the office?

One big reason most Christian men stay silent before friend and foe alike is that they're not sure they have the message right. Sure, it's in their hearts, but somehow it loses coherence on the way to their lips.

What if the other person starts asking questions I didn't anticipate? How much Bible knowledge is enough, anyway? And what about that verse that says there's "a time to be silent and a time to speak"? How will I know when the time is right?

These are precisely the questions I want to help you answer. Maybe you're never going to stroll up to a pulpit in Madison Square Garden, but you need to be able to wisely take advantage of the opportunities coming your way right now. The question is, how does this wisdom ever come?

Does God give you visions and dreams, like He gave to Abraham and his great-grandson Joseph? Do you get zapped while driving to church, the way Saul did on the road to Damascus? Do you wake up one morning having had your love for quarter-pounders with cheese suddenly replaced by a burning desire to go on a fast and research the book of Numbers?

Pilgrim's Progress

Actually, profound spiritual change usually comes in the same way as physical change. I've never looked into the bathroom mirror and been shocked to see someone very different from the man I saw the day before. From week to week my hair stays the same color, and the wrinkles seem to stay put. But once in a while I'll take a look at a photo from ten years back and—*aaack!* My beard wasn't gray, and the wrinkles were much fewer and less severe. And I was thinner!

The Holy Spirit works in us at about the same pace. He teaches, guides, corrects, always leading us forward one day at a time. Unfortunately the dramatic, quick-change testimonies lead many men to think that rapid transformation is *always* God's will, while anything less is a sign of carnality.

Then, already feeling inferior, they look inward and see His work in their own lives in purely *subtractive* terms: He takes away this bad habit, removes that ugly personality trait, purges that sinful desire. They think in terms of "purification" and "correction." They tend to see the Holy Spirit's ministry as one of continual reproof rather than constant progress. Yet *progress* expresses perfectly His daily objective in our lives.

Reproof *is* included in what He does, of course, but only as a step forward. Does an orchard owner prune a tree because he wants a smaller one? No, he wants more fruit—he wants progress! And he knows that progress comes slowly. Orchard owners are a patient lot. *So is the Holy Spirit.*

Here's some friendly advice as you prepare to take a more public stand for Christ: Be happy to be a work in progress! Don't be self-satisfied with where you are, but don't feel guilty for where you're not. You're still breathing, which means God hasn't given up on you! Cooperate with the Holy Spirit as He transforms you gradually, steadily, on a day-to-day basis.

The Terms of Surrender

You can also take comfort in understanding the true balance of power between you and any person who needs the Lord. *In every situation, at all times, you have the advantage.* It's based on certain facts that are not open to question. While you need not state these facts openly, you should *always* formulate your actions with unbelievers in light of them.

- God isn't on trial. He's the Judge.
- You aren't on trial. You're a witness.
- The Holy Spirit is the invisible Prosecutor (John 16:7–11).
- The one on trial is the man or woman whose sin requires a payment he or she is not capable of making (Hebrews 9:22; Colossians 1:13–14).
- A guilty verdict has already been reached (Romans 2:14–15, Colossians 2:13–14). Therefore, since there's nothing to "prove," you only have to tell the truth about God's method of forgiveness, which is *inherently* powerful

enough to pierce the unbelieving heart (Hebrews 4:12).
- All sinners have been sentenced and are already legally dead (Ephesians 2:1–5 and Colossians 2:13). What they crave is escape from this death—into new life from above.
- The only reason to convene this "lawsuit" is that God, by His grace, has decided to offer an already condemned sinner history's most merciful terms of *surrender*, as follows: Christ Jesus has decided to step forward and offer His blood as full payment, provided we admit our guilt and surrender unconditionally, acknowledging and confessing the reality of Jesus' resurrection and lordship. In return, God promises to raise us to new life in Christ, free from condemnation and further slavery to sin.

It's a pretty lopsided contest, isn't it? No wonder Paul called us "more than conquerors." No wonder he confidently told a little church in Rome that "the God of peace will soon crush Satan under your feet" (Romans 16:20). And that's exactly what happened! During the next couple of hundred years—even though it was illegal for Christians to meet for worship—Roman citizens came to Christ in ever-increasing numbers. Eventually Rome replaced Jerusalem as the governmental center of the Christian world, while the mighty Caesars and their worshipers ate, drank, and fiddled their pagan empire into oblivion.

If such a transformation took place in Rome, it can happen again—in Russia, South Africa, China, even on the street where you live! Neighborhoods, like nations, are baptized one person at a time.

Don't be fooled. The odds are never against you, because there are no odds. There are only facts. And the facts say "every knee will bow." It's just a matter of time, time that happens to be on our side.

All Work, No Pray

Along with perpetual guilt for not "witnessing," Christian men suffer a lot of unneeded stress and anxiety about two other stereotyped subjects. I've mentioned them before. They are

- Spending time with the Lord
- Spending time in God's Word.

Let's start with the former. How much time should the average Christian devote to worship and prayer? One South American minister gave a great answer to that question when a starry-eyed admirer showered him with compliments about his spirituality.

"Oh pastor, you must spend lots of time with God," she gushed. "Tell me, how much time do you spend alone with the Lord?"

"Well, let me think," he replied. "Right now, you and I and God are in this room together. But when you leave, I suppose I'll be alone with Him. *Hmmm*, I've never really added up all those moments."

Now that's a *truly* spiritual answer to a falsely spiritual question! Time with God isn't only made up of intense devotionals and weighty petitions, any more than marriage consists of constant lovemaking and heart-to-heart talks. Sure, those are important ingredients in the relationship, but they aren't the *essence* of it.

If you asked me to describe my typical day, I might tell you that I ran errands during the morning and afternoon and worked around the house all evening. Does that mean I didn't give any time to my family? Not at all. In fact, my wife and I did all these things together, but I didn't emphasize that fact, simply because her presence in my life is a given. I didn't even think to mention it, because with us one-plus-one equals one!

Realize that God's presence in your life is a given. Jesus promised to be with you always, to never leave you or forsake you (Hebrews 13:5). That means you're always together, that you're "one" with Him. Sure, you can talk to Him, anytime, anywhere. But you can also "think" to Him, leaving your mind open like the kitchen doors and windows when you're working on the patio and your wife is inside cooking.

Not only does such an attitude help keep your mind clean and uncluttered, but when it's time for one of those important discussions with God, you won't be hounded by guilt. Instead you'll be able to

> Enter his gates with thanksgiving and his courts with praise; give thanks to him and praise his name (Psalm 100:4).

Worshiping God precedes all other service to Him. And your relationship with Him, when it's healthy, quite naturally gives birth to serving Him in other ways.

Let me make it even clearer: Until you've learned to *enjoy* Him, you'll never enjoy representing Him. If your conscience is already dogging you before you ever start talking *to* Him, then your face and voice will surely show it when you try to talk *about* Him. At best you'll sound like Honest John, the used car salesman, trying to pass off a clunker as a good deal. At worst you'll dismiss yourself as a hypocrite and just never bring God into conversations.

Think back to the Christians you've known. Which ones were your favorites just for hanging around? Were they theologians? Evangelists? More likely they were the ones who seemed to really *know* God, as though they considered Him their closest friend. And they made *you* feel that way when you were around them. Sure, Billy Graham is a hero to many Christians, but ask a few of them to name the biggest godly influence in their lives and you'll hear more about Grandma than Graham. Why? Because although she couldn't preach and didn't pastor any presidents, she loved her little ones, served a great cookie with milk, and prayed for them when they skinned their knees. One thing millions of kids can be sure of: Grandma knows God.

Knowing God and enjoying Him are more important than becoming a great talker. They're more important to God, more important for your well-being, and more important in your witness to others, whether spoken or unspoken. Even though you may not preach like Billy, you can know God like Grandma.

Such a healthy relationship with the Lord puts the matter of serving Him into proper perspective. Otherwise, you'll either remain guilt-ridden and ineffective, or you'll become an "evange-holic" and weird out. Either way you'll eventually crash and burn and wind up on spiritual disability leave.

Stop reading for a minute and just talk to the Lord. If you feel guilty about not praying more, start with "I feel guilty for not praying more." If you don't know what to say, begin with "I don't know what to say." *If you feel unworthy, that's all the more reason to start!* And when a minute passes . . . start reading again, but keep the line to God open.

As for spending "enough" time in prayer, be careful that you don't start measuring it in *quantities*. Jesus warned us about this approach when He said, "And when you pray, do not keep on babbling like pagans, for they think they will be heard because of their many words" (Matthew 6:7).

This doesn't mean we shouldn't "ask and keep on asking," as the Lord commanded in the very next chapter (Matthew 7:7, *The Amplified Bible*). It is simply a warning to keep prayer in the realm of *relationship*, as opposed to turning it into some sort of intercessory frequent-flier program for accumulating spiritual miles.

The Bible: News You Can Use

What about that other haunting question: How much Bible knowledge is required for a guy like you? I'll admit that it's easy to be intimidated, especially when you see some eleven-volume commentary on a seven-page New Testament epistle. So many books have been written, so many sermons preached. What's the standard for a guy who works hard all week long, doesn't have time to go to seminary, and just wants to be able to answer an old friend's questions about God?

There's no point in hinting around at this. Bible study is a requirement for Christians, not an option. But most Christian men find it taxing on a daily basis. Consequently they either restrict their time in God's Word to some little promise book, or they just put it off altogether. Naturally, the promise book is good, but it no more substitutes for serious reading than a donut and coffee take the place of a balanced meal. How can the Holy Spirit guide us into "all truth" if we just consider truth a snack food?

Still, we're a generation that has grown up on newspapers, magazines, and half-hour TV sitcoms, so we find it difficult to read more than a chapter or two in a sitting . . . or a week . . . or a month. Frankly, a lot of men just won't read anything unless it's published twelve times a year in color and comes with a free "baseball bloopers" video.

But don't be depressed. There are understandable reasons why you don't read your Bible like you should. If you're the typical Christian man:

- You read the Scriptures for "spiritual guidance" rather than practical instruction.
- No matter how much you read, you just don't understand a lot of it.
- You have no idea how much Bible knowledge is "enough" for a working man, so you're intimidated from the moment you start reading.

I want to address your need and mine to get into Scripture as a lifestyle, not just to find "proof-texts" for defending your faith.

Here are five rules—I don't really like the word "rules," but we'll use it—that will help you to see the Scriptures as the practical manual it was meant to be.

Rule Number One

Read your Bible just like you read today's newspaper, as practical information concerned with the real world. Quit looking to achieve some inner glow; this is news you can use!

For example, the Fifth Commandment says to "Honor your father and your mother, so that you may live long in the land the LORD your God is giving you" (Exodus 20:12). You can meditate all day long on that verse, searching for "warm fuzzies" of enlightenment and inspiration. But it is simply an important, practical commandment, with a wonderful promise attached for those who obey it, and a cold, hard warning implied for those who don't. Read it again. It simply shows that a long and blessed life begins with honoring those who gave you life. Enjoying the future begins with respect for the past. It could just as easily have been phrased, "Do unto your parents as you someday would have your children do unto you." The flip-side? The man who fails to honor his parents will likely also fail to teach his children to do the same. He may be buying misery on a lay-away plan.

Rule Number Two

Read the Bible by the authors' division points, not the chapter and verse partitions, which translators later added. These scholars often started or ended passages in odd places. For example, Ephesians 5:22 through 6:9 is a complete section about families, which easily could be considered its own chapter. Read it that way, and you'll see what I mean.

Several newer editions of the Bible have dealt with this problem by grouping verses into naturally flowing paragraphs. Get one!

Rule Number Three

Always be open to the big picture—life in Christ—when you read God's Word. Don't let yourself get lost in Exodus or numbed by Numbers. They were written to reveal to you His character, and to establish you in His ways.

The overarching theme of the Bible is God's covenantal relationship with man. This means that even those musty old laws in Leviticus and Deuteronomy ultimately were written as practical instruction on Christian living. The apostle Paul was confident enough of this fact to claim that a passage about oxen was really a lesson to Christians about proper payment for services rendered.

> For it is written in the Law of Moses: "Do not muzzle an ox while it is treading out the grain." Is it about oxen that God is concerned? Surely he says this for us, doesn't he? Yes, this was written for us, because when the plowman plows and the thresher threshes, they ought to do so in the hope of sharing in the harvest. (1 Corinthians 9:9–10; see also 1 Timothy 5:17–18 regarding Paul's claim that good pastors deserve bigger salaries!)

Never forget what Paul knew so well: The Old Testament is all about the New Covenant!

Rule Number Four

Don't individualize every Scripture you read. The Bible was written to a *people*, not a person. So many Christians get tripped up trying to individually appropriate promises that were written to God's people as a community. For example, Joe Christian sees God's promise in Deuteronomy 28:13 to make His people "the head, not the tail," and takes it as God's will that a promotion is inevitable at work. Then, after he's been laid off, he's not only worried about his financial future, but he's also plagued in his mind and heart with accusations that his faith must be defective.

In truth, that Scripture, like so many others, was written as a promise of corporate blessing for corporate obedience to God's commandments. In other words, when faithfulness becomes a social trend, blessing multiplies! Likewise, when disobedience is the cultural rule of thumb, widespread suffering is sure to follow (often even afflicting the few good people who may live among the wicked majority).

Psalm 150 says to praise God with stringed instruments,

flute, and trumpet, but that doesn't mean everyone has to take lessons. It simply means *somebody* in the community of believers should.

As you study, keep in mind that you're one member in a whole body. You'll never understand every word, any more than you can fulfill every prophecy or claim every blessing. Which leads us to our last rule . . .

Rule Number Five

Don't worry about trying to walk in light you haven't seen. Just be confident in what you know, and honest about what you don't know. Don't be afraid to say, "I'm stumped," when you're stumped. And keep reading!

Remember, I'm not saying you have to become a theologian in a hard-hat. In truth, only God knows how much knowledge is "enough," because the answer is always changing as you grow. The "path of the just" is getting brighter and brighter like the rising sun, as the Holy Spirit transforms us day by day. Sure, the world could use a few more good theologians. But an auto mechanic who can intelligently comment on the Ten Commandments is as valuable to the cause of Christ as any wise man hunched over a Hebrew manuscript in some light-deprived library.

Doing What Comes Naturally

What about this matter of knowing when to speak up and when to keep quiet? The question, itself, usually means that you're still looking at "witnessing" as a duty, a presentation, a collection of techniques and approaches. But here again, the answer lies in relationship, not just with the Lord, but with the people in your life.

Hey, I know you don't have time to make a close friend out of every person in your neighborhood, office, and son's Little League bleachers. So who could? Even Jesus maintained only a few close friendships.

I'm simply advising you to honestly be the man God has made you, no more and no less, and to let the people around you watch His continuing work in you. When the Bible says "the righteous will live by his faith" (Habakkuk 2:4, cf. Romans 1:17), it's talking about the *richness* of the believer's lifestyle, not the artificiality of it. A life of faith includes talking to people about God, sure, but it also includes brushing your teeth, going to the store, working in the office, playing with your kids, even sleeping. In other words, living by faith means *living* by faith!

Think of your public stand for Christ as being like a roadside fruit stand. It's open to inspection all day long, and if the goods on display are appealing, somebody with an appetite is going to buy something. If the owner wants to stay open, he'll stock the place with fresh fruit again tomorrow, not only for repeat customers, but also in the hopes of attracting the guy who passed him by yesterday.

Now this guy could put out artificial fruit, the plastic kind, and initially draw a big crowd. Artificial fruit often looks better than the real thing. But most people would leave angry, never to return, and might even warn their friends to stay away from the place.

Real fruit is better.

He might also put the unsold items from yesterday on display again today. But fewer people will stop as the days wear on and the flies multiply.

Fresh fruit is better.

"But the fruit of the Spirit is love, joy, peace, patience, kindness, goodness, faithfulness, gentleness and self-control. Against such things there is no law" (Galatians 5:22–23).

Notice the Bible says the fruit of the Spirit "is," not "are." That's important. Those nine wonderful qualities are all aspects of one bountiful work of the Holy Spirit. Together they make for a well-balanced, well-integrated personality. And like apples and oranges, spiritual fruit isn't ingrown. It hangs right out there where people can see it, pick it, taste it. Where it can plunk them on the head once in a while when they get up close!

On the other hand, trying to work on peace this week, and kindness or patience next week while maintaining this week's peace, really complicates matters. It makes the Christian life as hard as trying to juggle nine balls when only one ball is available. In other words, it's both pointless and impossible.

Besides, trees don't "try" to grow fruit! Fruit is the product of a tree's *nature*. Yes, I know we have a fallen nature, and I'm not claiming that any of us is "naturally" godly. But I *am* saying that the Holy Spirit works to gradually change our nature, which is what Paul meant when he told us to "be transformed by the renewing of your mind. Then you will be able to test and approve what God's will is—his good, pleasing and perfect will" (Romans 12:2b).

Transformed! Renewed minds! Now that's progress! Yet to listen to some folks, you'd think the Bible instructed us to be transformed by the *removal* of our minds.

- "Oh, I never watch television or even read the newspaper. I just read my Bible." I see . . . and did it tell you about the seven inches of snow predicted for your garage sale tomorrow?
- "Well, my physical man didn't feel anything, but my spirit-man really bore witness." And I'll bet your soul is in line at McDonald's, buying lunch for the three of you.
- "Man, that guy was all over the platform when he preached. He was really in the Spirit!" Yeah, maybe. But being in the Spirit doesn't have to mean acting like he's out of his mind.

Look, I don't want to poke fun at a man whose sermon style is better than mine, or at someone whose faith doesn't depend on sensory stimulus. But it's important to remind ourselves that there's no point in trying to be more spiritual than God! Jesus didn't die to deliver us from being human, or to make us divine, but to redeem our humanity by letting us partake of His divine nature (2 Peter 1:4).

This is why we're called the *people* of God. Redeemed people are *real* people, saved in order to fulfill God's original purpose in creating man: To know and love Him, to keep His commandments and represent Him to the world.

You don't have to be perfect in order to stand up for Christ. You just have to be real. So if you're living, breathing, learning, and imperfect but wanting to improve, then you can quietly start taking a stand for Christ right now.

For Thought and Discussion

1. What sections of the Bible do you normally skip? Why? How could you go about studying these sections—what materials could help you?
2. When could you fit Bible study—on your own or in a group—into your schedule?
3. When could you fit a regular time for prayer into your schedule?

All in the Family:
Taking a Stand With Unbelieving Family Members

This isn't something to be proud of, but I've hardly ever been caught speechless. I've talked my way past Soviet immigration officers, addressed countless American high-school audiences, and spoken to spitball-tossing socialists at a Spanish university, all without want for words. In fact, I can only recall being consistently speechless in one setting, and it had nothing to do with platforms or police. Instead it involved standing before someone far more intimidating than the KGB. I had to face my dad.

My father had pastored for thirty-one years when he rebelled against the Lord in his early fifties. Suddenly the man who had trained me to follow in his footsteps didn't want to hear a thing I had to say. My life and ministry, which had always been a testimony to his own, now seemed an indictment instead. For five years I choked and sputtered through our visits, knowing that one wrong remark, one little hint of calling him to repentance, might spark an angry explosion.

What can you do when your own father is running from the Lord? What do you say to a wife who has never had much reason to respect you spiritually? Forget winning souls in Af-

rica. How does a man stand up for Christ in his own household?

The bonds of family are powerful and unique. On the one
hand, we're closer to family members than to anyone else on
earth. We talk about things behind closed doors that we'd
never say in front of the world. On the other hand, this very
closeness can quickly become an emotional electric fence,
charged from both sides with all the reasons why we absolutely *cannot* talk about God.

Here are a few of the spoken or unspoken defenses you may
encounter:

- Religion has always been a taboo subject around here. Let's
  keep it that way.
- Just because you've "found God" doesn't mean the whole
  family has to get religion.
- Since when did *you* become Mr. Perfect?

The tension causes you to have second thoughts of your
own.

- I'm the last person my father (wife, son) would ever listen
  to.
- My son already thinks I'm a dictator.
- I'm not exactly Mr. Perfect to begin with.

Thus the looming prospect of rejection and general un-
pleasantness keeps many men silent about life in Christ. They
don't want to put someone they love through an emotional
wringer; after all, their desire is to share joy, not pain.

Isn't it ironic? Sometimes the greatest happiness you've
ever known seems hardest to communicate to the people you
love most. Joy causes pain. Closeness becomes distance. It
wouldn't be so bad if a stranger didn't want to listen, or if you
were told to keep away by somebody you didn't like in the first
place. But it's terribly frustrating to be shut out by someone
you love.

What a dilemma! It hurts to keep quiet about something so

wonderful and eternally important, but it also hurts to talk about it. Any way you look at it, conflict seems inevitable.

Well, I want to show you how to relieve some of the pain, and how to avoid certain kinds of distress altogether. But let's not kid around, either. This business of knowing Jesus is a matter of life and death: life for those who surrender to His lordship, and death for those who don't. In other words, the anguish that results from *not* sharing one's faith in Christ is ultimately much greater than any domestic discomfort suffered when loving concern bumps into I'd-rather-not-talk-about-it.

Love Hurts

Jesus knew He was putting you and a lot of other folks in this particular pickle by showing up to redeem the world.

> Do you think I came to bring peace on earth? No, I tell you, but division. From now on there will be five in one family divided against each other, three against two and two against three. They will be divided, father against son and son against father, mother against daughter and daughter against mother, mother-in-law against daughter-in-law and daughter-in-law against mother-in-law (Luke 12:51–53).

Division—son against father, mother against daughter— these were the unavoidable effects of Christ's mission. Sure they were troublesome, even agonizing. After all, love was His motivation too. But whereas you and I probably would have avoided potential conflicts in the name of caring, He marched right into them *because* He cared. In fact, it was Love that enabled Jesus to put aside the fear of rejection. And unlike you and I, He *knew* He would be rejected (with a bit more severity than the slamming of a kitchen door, I might add).

The Lord's example puts things in perspective, doesn't it? It isn't really love that keeps us from standing up for Christ around our parents, siblings, wives, and children. It's fear. Fear of rejection. Fear of confrontation. Fear of getting tongue-tied. And perhaps more than any other, the fear of having to live up to the high standard we invoke by bringing Him into the picture.

One of the biggest reasons why most Christian men tremble at the thought of witnessing to their own families is that those are the people who know them so well. They can smell the slightest hint of baloney on their breath.

Remember when your mom told you to brush your teeth and get ready for bed? As a ten-year-old you usually didn't have the patience to stand in front of the sink or anything else for longer than fifteen seconds, so you'd often just rub the dry brush as far as your canines a couple of times and then dart back into the living room. Sometimes you got away with it, but sometimes Mom would check your work. She'd ask if you brushed, and you would nod yes, while self-consciously closing your mouth (a dead give-away). You were afraid she would smell your unwashed breath.

In fact—and here's the real point—even if you used toothpaste and water, working up your lathery rabid dog impression in the mirror, sometimes you still were afraid that you hadn't done it right. Good enough for you might not be good enough for Mom.

Twenty or thirty years later you've got your brushing down, but there are so many other areas in your life that still aren't good enough. You think you have bad spiritual breath. Or you fear that there's some small piece of ethical lettuce stuck between your teeth, which is going to put everybody off the minute you open your mouth about the Lord.

So you clamp those lips together one more time and tell yourself you're still not good enough to pass inspection. Yes-sir, you've got a lot of flossing to do before you can turn those pearly whites into the Pearly Gates. Maybe you can't be Mr. Perfect, you tell yourself, but you've got to try, or else your family will never listen.

The Perfectionism of Saints

I heard a clever sermon title not long ago. My sister's pastor preached on "Turning Isms Into Wasms," the initial premise being that some people's lives are ruled by isms: idealism, escapism, fanaticism, and the like. Isms are usually good concepts taken to extremes, literally "too much of a good thing." Community, for example, is a biblical ideal, but recent history confirms the horrors of communism. Liberality is a godly trait, encouraged by Scripture. Liberalism, however, often presages the collapse of a culture. Femininity is a wonderful quality in a woman. But feminism, well. . . ?

One of the most insidious isms ever to snake its way into the lives of Christians is a doctrine of demons called *perfectionism*. It's one that most Christians don't officially believe, but many slavishly practice. Perfectionism is the belief that moral and/or spiritual perfection is achievable in this life. The stepchild of guilt and fear, it is probably the number one bogeyman stifling the average Christian man's witness at home.

Perfectionism is a seductive substitute for honesty, the ground in which all Christian living should be rooted. Why? Because honesty is too quickly attainable. It's not only possible, but possible *right now*, and that means no more excuses for not getting down to the business of talking to Dad about his eternal soul. It's impossible, however, to become perfect. And if Satan can keep me striving for something impossible, he can silence me permanently.

Besides, flawlessness was never all it's cracked-up to be. Ezekiel's symbolic king of Tyre is a "perfect" example.

"You were blameless in your ways from the day you were created till wickedness was found in you" (Ezekiel 28:15).

Bible commentators can't decide if this Scripture is about Lucifer or Adam, but as vices go you wouldn't want to be either one anyway. In both cases the two essentially aspired to the same idolatrous height: "I will make myself like the Most

High" (Isaiah 14:14b). Satan wanted to replace God, and Adam wanted to be his own god.

Perfectionism pushes you to commit our original grandpa's iniquity, to pluck another apple from the same old tree. It forces you not to be godly, but to try to "be like the Most High." It depicts salvation as an intimidating achievement, rather than a work of God's grace that tells a secretly hungry heart, "This could happen to you, too."

Needless to say, this Trojan horse carries a bellyful of attackers, just waiting to spring into action. Once perfectionism has invaded the conscience, then condemnation, compulsion, legalism, and a host of other spiritual viruses can tyrannize a Christian of almost any stripe.

- A young midwestern father won't take his baby boy to the doctor because it would show a lack of faith in God for healing.
- An old Chicago grandpa can never light enough candles or count enough beads. Perpetual penance is the price exacted by a lifetime of never being good enough.
- A twice-married businessman knows his younger brother's marriage will fall apart soon if he doesn't turn to God. But he also knows the brother doesn't want to hear about Christ from him, so he clams up. Then he helplessly watches a whole family crash and burn.

Have I found you yet?

Perfectionism says you'd better be sure you can close every sale before you ever *start* witnessing. It turns what ought to be the joy of sharing your very soul into the stress of a boardroom presentation, complete with charts (Bible verses), memorized opening lines, and a good supply of antacid.

The pressure becomes especially intense when taking a stand for Christ in front of family members, because they know your faults. In fact, the only person who knows your shortcomings as well is you. For every loved one who needs the Lord, you can name a deficiency that disqualifies you from being the one to discuss it with him.

- Your dad had to help you tunnel through a mountain of debt. Why should he think you're any better with souls than you've been with money?
- Your brother was always smarter and stronger than you. Why should he listen to you now?
- Your wife can't even get you to exercise. Why should she go to church with you?
- Your daughter grew up hearing the arguments through the bedroom wall. Why should she want to pray with you?

No doubt about it. It's going to take a *lot* of work before you can ever bring up knowing God to this bunch. You'll have to get completely out of debt, move up to senior management, lose forty pounds, memorize the book of Romans, go five years without a fight at home, make a few good investments, and fix the front fence. Then they'll want to hear about the Lord, right?

No. But maybe they'll come to visit you at the rest home.

I Exalt Me, I Exalt Me

Look, there's nothing wrong with wanting to set a good example. But thinking you have to be perfect, or even nearly perfect, in front of your family only means that you've made yourself rather than Jesus the standard of justification. In other words, you're busy trying to get them to accept you rather than Him!

But you can't testify to your righteousness and His at the same time. You can only give witness to *His righteousness in you*. This is what the apostle Paul meant when he said:

> I have been crucified with Christ and no longer live, but Christ lives in me. The life I live in the body, I live by faith in the Son of God, who loved me and gave himself for me (Galatians 2:20).

A few years ago, while in London, England, my wife and I went to watch the changing of the guard at Buckingham Palace. As we stood in front of the massive iron gates, I thought about the huge crowds that gather there whenever the Queen is in royal procession. Everyone waves to her: adults, children, old folks, rich and poor, even the pickpocket with one hand raised. They all honor Her Majesty. Why? Because the procession is all about *her* worth, not theirs.

Your family's need of Christ has nothing to do with what you have to offer, other than your total honesty about His grace and goodness toward you. What you want to show them is *His* worth. And the way to do that is to be truthful about His work in you, about your struggles as well as your successes.

Of course, this means letting them see you as you really are. It means being honest, which in turn requires being vulnerable, and that scares many men. But it's still easier than being perfect. Granted, it implies a kind of nakedness, a concept most men find attractive in the bedroom but mortifying in spiritual matters. We fear baring our souls the way, as kids, we used to fear baring our behinds to a doctor with a hypodermic. But the lesson of childhood holds true: The anticipation hurts a lot more than the needle!

Don't try to hide your weaknesses. Your family is familiar with them anyway. Rather you should glory—not indulge, but glory—in them. Even though Paul probably was writing about physical infirmity, his lesson from the Lord holds true for our purposes.

> But he said to me, "My grace is sufficient for you, for my power is made perfect in weakness." Therefore I will boast all the more gladly about my weaknesses, so that Christ's power may rest on me. That is why, for Christ's sake, I delight in weaknesses, in insults, in hardships, in persecutions, in difficulties. For when I am weak, then I am strong (2 Corinthians 12:9–10).

You'll be a much more effective Christian, and a lot happier to boot, just letting your loved ones see that you're still yourself, or more accurately, that you're *finally* yourself. Let them watch you in process, as you submit to the Holy Spirit's work in your life. Let them be inspired by a true "artist at work," as He chisels away the stony facade of all that inherited sin, and reveals the real, redeemable you.

They still won't see a perfect man, at least not on this side of heaven. But you can let them see God's *perfect work* (Deuteronomy 32:4) as He performs it in you.

And remember, no matter how hard you try, being anything other than what you really are is not a witness. It's a lie.

Doing Unto Others

Some men, of course, aren't so demanding of themselves. On the contrary, they rejoice in the fact that, even though they're not perfect, they've been forgiven! These are the guys who start spreading their joy around from the moment they receive it. After all, the peace in their hearts is exactly what their beloved families need.

Unfortunately some of these men dispense the Good News the way Jim Jones distributed Kool-Aid® to his followers. Their gospel is laced with condescension, poisoned by condemnation. This kind of perfectionist gives his pressure-laden son a sermon when he needs a friend. He gives his hurting daughter a Scripture-peppered pep-talk instead of a hug.

Perfectionism, you see, doesn't just come in the "me" flavor. There's also the variety that wants to perfect *you*. I know about it, because I used to dish it out by the mouthful during my early twenties, the time in my life that's best described as my "obnoxious-for-Jesus" period.

I was into books on faith and positive attitude, books that have enriched many people's lives, but which I used as billy clubs on myself and those around me. I was never sick; I just had lying symptoms. My vocabulary didn't allow me to admit I was coming down with a cold; rather I was catching a healing. Christian men didn't attend retreats; they went to "advances." (Actually I still kind of like that one.)

I had been a missionary with a musical gospel team for all of one-and-a-half years when I went home to Maryland for four months. Great things had taken place during our team's year-long mission to South Africa. Thousands of people, primarily teenagers, had come to the Lord, and were enrolled in Bible correspondence courses. We had packed auditoriums and stadiums with both black and white audiences, even integrating many meetings, which was an unusual victory in 1970. Our records were being played on national radio, and we were soon to be invited to sing for the Billy Graham crusade during our return trip the next year. In short, everything I could have asked from God, and more, was happening. And that was due, I thought, to the fact that He was honoring my positive confession and attitude.

Now I was back in Baltimore, with Dad and Mom and four brothers and sisters in their middle and preteens. I was the third adult in the house, a minister like Dad, and my little brother's hero. We all loved each other a lot, and I was sure my whole family would want to learn the great spiritual formulas I was quickly mastering. All they needed was some healing encouragement when they coughed, or a little reminder whenever they committed a slip of the tongue. This would be four months of victory for all of us.

Wrong. Little sisters don't like constant correction. And fathers positively hate it! Within days I had offended everyone except my kid brother, Kevin, and maybe André, our poodle. I still remember my day of reckoning, still hear the sound of Dad's hand slamming the table, the plates and silverware jumping, as he called me a holier-than-thou. Everyone else got up right away, sensible enough to know that dinner had just been adjourned. I sat there alone, smarting, with a stunned "whud-I-do?" look on my face.

Even Mom, the peacemaker, winced in agreement with him. That made it official. Like the man who considered himself a great hunter but was really the guy who shot Bambi's mother, I was a jerk.

I had only wanted to help. One of the twins had made a pessimistic remark, and I had tried to force-feed her a bit of encouragement. But my "advice" sent her into tears, prompting a loud complaint from her sister. Dad had heard enough. (So had God.)

My parents and siblings, by God's grace, were long on patience and quick with forgiveness. But my sisters soon entered a stage of mild midteen rebellion, and my "encouragement" during those months probably helped push them away from the Lord rather than toward Him. Within a short time, thank God, He brought them back to himself, but He did it without my help.

Such "other-oriented perfectionism," as experts call it, isn't rooted in love so much as ambition. It defeats every goal a man sets for ministry at home. And in the minds of unbelieving loved ones, it reinforces the all-too-common image that being a Christian means changing oneself *for* a very demanding God rather than being changed *by* a very gracious God. Moreover, in many cases it is the outgrowth of unresolved self-oriented perfectionism. In other words, the insecure pot is calling the unsaved kettle black.

What to Do

The Saturn Corporation bills itself as "a different kind of car company." What's different about it? For one thing, at the dealership a potential customer can browse the floor and look at cars without having a salesman on his coattail asking questions designed to reel him in. Has this strategy worked? Thus far hundreds of thousands of Saturn buyers have decided that it was worth paying a higher price in order to avoid some pushy Honest John, who may or may not have been offering a good deal on another brand of automobile.

Saturn's sales credo, to state it tersely, simply instructs the sales force to "shut up and back off." That's precisely the right kind of advice for the man of too many words who wants to take a stand for Christ with his family.

Fewer words and more respect will go a long way toward opening closed ears and hearts. That's because fewer words and more respect involve listening, something a lot of us have forgotten how to do, which makes it that much more important, especially at home.

"But my kids won't talk to me, at least not about anything sensitive or serious." Well, maybe they won't at first, especially if they think it will bring on a sermon. But that's okay. Most of us went for years without talking to God, but He kept demonstrating His love for us "while we were still sinners" (Romans 5:8). He kept listening to our complaining, aching hearts, even when we only used His name as a curse word. Now we've got to do the same thing for our loved ones. We must demonstrate the love of Christ, who loves them just as they are right now.

The Bible says to honor our parents—it doesn't specify that they must be Christians to qualify. Ephesians 5:25 says to love our wives, not set our sights on changing them. Chapter six says to admonish our children without exasperating them. That means bringing correction, but not in a way that invites rebellion.

Maybe your dad wasn't a very good one. Maybe your teenager doesn't seem to respect himself, you, or anyone else. Maybe your wife has become withdrawn, because constant attempts to "encourage" her have left her convinced that she isn't valued or respected for who she is. Well, now it's time to

- Be a better husband simply because you love your wife, not because you're trying to earn the right to witness to her.
- Ask your parents for their opinions because they give good advice, not because it means they'll then be obligated to listen to you talk about God.
- Take your daughter to dinner, not because you want to talk

her into going to church, but because you two need each other right now, exactly as you are.

Maybe my hypothetical examples don't fit your situation, but you see the point I'm making. Your family is God's blessing to you, here and now, in their present condition. And you're a special gift from God to them, a sign of His favor to them, because Christ in you is their "hope of glory."

The best thing you can do for them is to give them the same kind of breaks that the Lord has always given you. God's love may have haunted you, but He didn't harass you. When you blew it a thousand times, He didn't harangue you with one-liners like "If you'd just give your life to Jesus this wouldn't happen anymore." No, instead He set about creating the optimal circumstances for your eventual surrender to Him.

I know you don't have command of the wind and waves, and you can't overwhelm your unsaved dad or daughter with a blinding light from heaven on the road to Damascus. But you can still create a climate of welcome for your loved ones, one where it's easier for them to run to you (and God) rather than away from you. And you do it not by indulging in the folly of perfectionism—neither the "me" nor "you" kind—but by being honest and open, by letting them watch God's Holy Spirit at work in your life.

Take a lesson from the Saturn Corporation. Forget trying to be the super salesman, and give them a chance to look at the product!

Honest to Goodness

Remember the first time your folks or an elementary school teacher impressed upon you the old saw, "honesty is the best policy"? They probably told you about Honest Abe Lincoln, and about George Washington, who chopped down his family's cherry tree, and how little George bravely faced his father's discipline with "I cannot tell a lie." Well, they were right.

Honesty *is* the best policy, and it's really at the heart of every-thing I've been promoting here. But don't get a wrong impression.

It might sound as though I've been encouraging you to just be caring and loving, and to take everything on the chin. But that's only two-thirds right; the chin part is wrong. Love is long-suffering, but it isn't passive. Love may "suffer all things," but honesty won't let it pretend nothing happened when something did. Love speaks the truth (Ephesians 4:15). Honesty is love's vocabulary.

The Lord didn't want to turn us into pasty-faced wimps when He gave one of His most famous commands.

> But I tell you who hear me: Love your enemies, do good to those who hate you, bless those who curse you, pray for those who mistreat you. If someone strikes you on one cheek, turn to him the other also. If someone takes your cloak, do not stop him from taking your tunic (Luke 6:27–29).

Jesus wasn't promoting passivity and pacifism when He said these things. Rather He was describing the ingenious action and intelligent aggression of God's love. One of my all-time-favorite bumper stickers puts it well: "Love your enemy. It'll drive him crazy." The Lord's reasoning was akin to an old military strategy, one that says it's sometimes worthwhile to lose a battle in order to win the war.

Taking a stand as a man of God in your home requires honesty, yes, and humility. But these are as tactically smart as they are spiritually pure. They're marks of strength, not weakness. If someone starts goading and testing you, you don't have to adopt the sniffling look of a Victorian spinster, too cultured and proper to suffer insults. This is all about redemptive strategies, not repressed psyches.

Sometimes God's love and wisdom *will* require you to turn the other cheek. It might mean gaining a brother later. Sometimes it's better to be silent, as Jesus was before Pilate (Matthew 27:14), while at other times "a gentle answer turns away wrath" (Proverbs 15:1). There also will be times when godly honesty requires that you speak up, like Paul when he invoked his Roman citizenship to the jailer who was about to scourge him (Acts 22:25). In that instance, the apostle's talkativeness got him a free ticket to Rome as well as the opportunity to tell Caesar about Jesus. He knew exactly what he was doing. He knew when to talk.

There's the key: knowing when to talk. I've just spent part of the time encouraging fearful men to talk, and the other part exhorting overbearing men to shut up. But the truth is there's "a time to be silent and a time to speak" (Ecclesiastes 3:7).

I can't tell you when it's wise to do one or the other at your house. I can only encourage you to incline your ear, humble your heart, and love your family the way God has loved you. One of the most wonderful things I've learned over the years is this: If people *know* you love them, you can say almost anything to them.

As for my dad, well, Mom was long-suffering, and we kids, since we couldn't correct him, concentrated on honoring him. He died a few years later, a happy husband and contented grandpa. He died a man of God.

Don't ever give up.

For Thought and Discussion

1. Are you simply trying to "grow" as a Christian—or are you laboring to become "perfect" before you share your faith with someone in your family?

2. Who are the toughest people in your family to talk to, when it comes to matters of faith? What's really keeping you from talking to them—your own sense of imperfection, or their verbal defenses?

3. How honest and vulnerable are you with your family about your "growth" areas? Would it gain you the right to be

heard if you were more genuine and humble in this area?
4. Do the people in your family know you love and care about them—or do they think you're just trying to change the "doctrinal lobe" of their brain?

5

Loving Thy Neighbor:
Taking a Stand With Old Friends

Joe Christian was a wild man back in college—not a criminal, mind you, but certainly a wild man. He was the kind who never missed a class or a party, but definitely missed a lot of sleep. He counted beer by the pitcher rather than by the can, once climbed a four-hundred-foot radio tower just to hang a frat-house banner, and spent his spring breaks at Daytona doing things he's tried hard to forget since coming to Christ.

Now Joe's a thirty-something father of three and leads one of his church's care groups every Thursday night at home. Except tonight. This Thursday he's back on the old campus across town, attending Homecoming.

He decided to go because lately he's missed seeing his old friends, even if they were a bad influence on him. What's more, he has felt a desire to let them know how God has changed him, since he was, no doubt, an equally bad influence on them. The contrast ought to be noticeable, and—he hopes—inviting. So here he is.

The problem is, beyond the little things like drinking iced tea instead of guzzling beer, Joe has no idea how to demonstrate the changes in his life. Should he speak right up and say,

"I don't appreciate those jokes anymore," or just let his silence speak for itself? What if his old buddies get embarrassed, or worse, offended by what they perceive as somebody who thinks he's too good for them now?

A similar situation exists with Joe's next-door neighbor, John Heathen. Joe also would like to share his Christian faith with John. But how? There's no big outward difference in their lives. He wishes God would do something spectacular in his life, something John could see as the undeniable hand of Providence. But it never happens. Their lives just keep running along parallel tracks: same Little League games, same PTA meetings, same colds in winter and weeds in spring.

Sadly, Joe knows that from John's perspective, the biggest difference in their lives is that the Heathen family has Sunday mornings free! So who has it better here? Why doesn't Joe's "good news" translate into any visible differences between him and the world around him?

Let's ask that question from John Heathen's point of view: What does Joe Christian have that John would want?

Joe's a nice guy. So is John.

Joe loves his wife and kids. So does John.

Joe works hard to make an honest living. So does John.

Joe has never cheated on his wife. Neither has John . . . as long as lust doesn't count.

Joe doesn't smoke. Ditto John, who quit two years ago.

Joe doesn't drink. Well, John doesn't get drunk, but he sure enjoys a couple of beers with his pizza, and appreciates a glass of fine wine with dinner. Poor Joe could be missing out here.

John goes down the list. There are movies Joe won't watch, jokes he won't laugh at, magazines he won't touch. He's against abortion and pornography and that kooky doctor up north who helps people commit suicide. In fact, it's pretty easy to name what Joe is *against*. The hard thing is figuring out what he's *for*. What does he believe in doing besides going to church? John draws a blank. He can't for the life of him see one real benefit in Joe's religion, other than going to heaven

when you die, but who really knows about the afterlife anyway?

Next door, Joe feels powerless and guilty. He knows that
being a nice guy without Christ won't cut it in eternity. Hell
is full of nice guys, and he wants to make sure John doesn't
join them. But he's stumped, caught in the same dilemma as
he is with his old schoolmates: How can he make John aware
of his need for Christ without putting his neighbor down or
sounding self-righteous?

How does a man take Jesus to Homecoming? How does he
stand up for Christ in conversation across his own backyard
fence? Sometimes it seems like it would be easier to take the
Gospel to Africa than to go next door!

Thou Shalt

The answer to Joe's questions lies in Leviticus 19:18, where
God originally gave the commandment to "love your neighbor
as yourself." Paul summarized the latter five of the Ten Commandments with this same phrase (see Romans 13:9–10), just
as Jesus did (see Matthew 22:39).

Have you ever asked yourself why *are* the Ten Commandments so full of negatives? Eight of them say "Thou shalt not"
do something or other. Does righteous living really boil down
to abstaining from what we're *not* supposed to do?

A lot of people think so, but they're wrong. And they per-
petuate the error by the boring lives they lead in the name of
Christian decency. This kind of thinking is also why so many
people view heaven as a cosmic retirement village where nobody has to work anymore, a welfare state where gold and di-
amonds are handed out like unemployment checks.

Actually many of God's laws were given in negative form
in order to properly restrict the power of civil government in
the lives of citizens. For example, "You shall not steal" (Exodus 20:15) meant the state could only prosecute theft. Hon-

estly acquired property was to be beyond their reach. (Says a lot about taxes, doesn't it?)

In reality, for every "thou shalt not" there are many "thou shalts." Every commandment stated in negative terms implies—in fact, demands—positive conduct from us as lovers of God and men. But that conduct is to be heartfelt rather than forced. It must be motivated by love rather than compelled by a government.

This opens up a whole world of possibilities when it comes to expressing true Christian love for those around us. It also relieves us of the truly unbiblical idea of interrupting, if not fracturing, friendships in the name of witnessing. On the contrary, true Christian love enables us to be better buddies and neighbors than ever before in a score of practical ways both big and small. For example, here's a good start for Joe in ministering to his old friends and next-door neighbors, the Heathens:

- He can make it a habit to thank God for their friendship during grace at their backyard cookouts. Such a gesture is welcoming rather than threatening, and it also gets Joe's friends used to being in the presence of people who pray. (We'll discuss this a bit more later.)
- The Christians can buy the Heathens a good-quality study Bible for Christmas, enclosing a little note that says something like, "The Book's a lot better than the movie. Hope you like it!" Joe could suggest a good place to start reading, as well.
- Joe and his wife can offer to baby-sit for the weekend of the Heathens' wedding anniversary. That way John and his wife can enjoy a nice, romantic break, while the Heathen kids get to watch a Christian family in action for forty-eight hours.

Surprise! None of these suggestions involves a confrontation or the performance of a miracle. But remember, a real witness is all about growing fruit, not raining manna. These sim-

ple acts involve giving and serving. They're neighborly, not
churchy, invitations made in driveways, not at altars. But they
may well lead to altars and, for the Heathen family, to God. In
any case, they're about *doing what we already know how to
do.*

How liberating! God doesn't *expect* you to do what He
hasn't *equipped* you to do. He knows on the one hand that you
aren't Billy Graham, and on the other that you can hook up
battery cables and change a car's oil in fifteen minutes, because that's more or less the way He made you. So He gives
you opportunities based on your abilities.

Do You Hear What I Hear?

My wife, Dolly, is the perfect example. She breaks into a
cold sweat at the very thought of any formal speaking presentation, whether in front of a crowd or one on one. That
rules out most evangelism programs right away. But she's
probably the greatest conversationalist that ever lived,
whether with a friend at lunch or with total strangers on the
phone. People often are telling her within ten minutes things
they wouldn't tell me after a year.

What's her secret? What great spiritual gift has God be-
stowed on her? Well, it's a rare one these days. *She listens.* She
listens and cares, and she lets people know they're worth her
time. The result is a life-changing ministry that spans conti-
nents.

"Yeah, but she's a woman, and they're always better at con-
versing than men. What's her example doing in a men's book?"
She's here for the same reason Esther and Ruth are in the
Bible. Because we can learn from her example. I know I am.

I've been a professional talker and thinker for almost three
decades, but for most of that time I haven't been a listener, not
in living and dining rooms anyway. Put somebody on television or behind a microphone and I hear them, if their subject
interests me, of course. But introduce me to your brother from

Des Moines, and my ears turn off during the handshake. It isn't that I don't care, it's just that I . . . uh . . . don't care!

It's the truth isn't it? We *don't* care, so we don't listen. That doesn't mean we're heartless brutes. The Super Bowl and the Final Four alone prove otherwise. But in an age when information assaults our senses all day long with everything from Iraqi news to old Beach Boys tunes, men have learned to turn the sound off in most non-business settings. Our files are full.

But if we're going to love our neighbors we've got to start caring, and that means listening. And Paul's prescription shows exactly where to start and what to listen for: "Love does no harm to its neighbor. Therefore love is the fulfillment of the law" (Romans 13:10).

What does he mean by love "fulfilling" the law? Is he saying that if you love somebody you're automatically satisfying God's requirements? No, not exactly. Actually Paul is saying that loving your neighbor means *consciously* keeping God's commandments. In other words, the commandments spell out specific ways of loving your neighbor.

I've already told you what a great listener my wife is. But how does listening fulfill any of the last five commandments? Well, let's look at the *positive* side of each.

- You shall not kill: That's about health and life—about the person himself.
- You shall not commit adultery: That's about marriage and family structure.
- You shall not steal: That's about ownership and making an honest living.
- You shall not bear false witness: That's about justice and a good reputation.
- You shall not covet: That's about one's estate, his present and future well-being.

Lives, families, jobs, reputations, and futures. These are everybody's biggest concerns, whether we're talking about old college chums or the family next door. They're also what Dolly asks about. She tunes-in on them like the stations on a radio dial.

Memorize these five commandments and you'll find yourself stunned at the opportunities for ministry already staring you in the face. And once people know you care enough to listen, you'll be amazed at how wide they'll open their hearts, not only to you but to the God you serve.

Let's look at some of them and be specific.

Hearers and Doers

The Seventh Commandment, the one about adultery, is concerned with marriage, which is the foundation of the home and ultimately of society itself. So how can you keep this one as a way of loving your neighbor?

Dolly and I capitalize on anniversaries, which commemorate marriages, and kids' birthdays, which celebrate the fruitfulness of marriage. For example, we buy Christian children's videos for our friends' little ones. The kids love them, and in no time at all they're prancing through the house singing songs about Jesus.

This, of course, is not only a wonderful way to plant seeds of righteousness in the heart of a child, but it's also a great way to get moms and dads to listen to the Gospel. Would *we* be welcome to sing those songs to them, especially fifteen times a day? Not on your life! But little Suzi can.

Purple dinosaur videos and Big Bird℠ dolls make good gifts, but wouldn't it be better to know your friends' children were singing about Jesus?

By the way, so far not a single dad and mom have objected to this kind of gift, no matter how unchristian the family might otherwise be. I think it's because they understand that our faith comes with our friendship: It's a package deal.

Then there's the Eighth Commandment, which says, "You shall not steal." Theft is an age-old substitute for work, which is the positive aspect of this law. So it ought to infer something about taking a stand for Christ in the marketplace.

Is a man's Christianity appropriate at the office? You bet! But since companies exist primarily to make good products and generate a profitable bottom line, your goals in loving your neighbors at work should start with the job itself.

Here's the first rule in standing up for Christ at work: Don't steal from your neighbors in the company by being less than fully productive. If you've let people know you're a Christian, then you've publicly committed yourself to the highest of standards in representing Him.

Jesus said to "let your light shine before men, that they may see your good deeds and praise your Father in heaven" (Matthew 5:16). Those good works include *work*! What the Lord is telling us is that, both on and off the job, *the quality of our deeds reflects His praises in a way that brings men to Him*. It follows then that mediocre work, or working with a bad attitude, doesn't really glorify Him at all.

As for when to talk with co-workers, or even the boss, about the Lord, lunchtime is a great time, especially if you're paying. Better yet, take time to be a true friend *after* work. After all, if you don't have time to clean a fish, you shouldn't be out there trying to catch him.

You'll notice I haven't even mentioned the old witnessing stand-by, keeping a Bible on your desk—or its '90s version, using a Scripture verse "screen saver" on your computer. They're fine too, even advisable in most instances. After all, you have a constitutional right to such free expression.

But you also have the promise of God's wisdom when you need it, and sometimes wisdom may dictate backing off if someone has complained or reacted negatively to a display of your faith. Remember, be willing to lose a battle in order to win a war.

The important thing is the spirit in which you do the things you do. Besides, I'll bet a guy who's been employee of the month for six months running could get away with John 3:16 on his PC pretty easily.

Is There Life After Work?

Let's punch the time clock and go home to look at another Commandment. The tenth one is a catch-all injunction against covetousness and, by implication, it promotes an open-door policy to your own happy abode. If ever there was a "neighbor" commandment, this is one.

Unfortunately we don't really have time to be friends with our friends and neighbors, do we? So many of us go to work in one part of town, take the kids to school in another part of town, attend church in yet another section, and live in a fourth. We just don't have any more time.

Or do we?

From the very first day God created until today, every day has been twenty-four hours long, given a leap-second here and there. We have as much time as anyone ever had. In fact, you might even say we have more, when you consider that Noah didn't have power tools and Moses didn't own a word processor. But we use our time differently. Or does it use us?

Nowadays it's different. We tend to let technology own us rather than us owning it. Our homes are electronic cocoons, with television, video games and computers keeping us from flesh-and-blood contact with the people around us. Even telephones, which enable us to "reach out and touch" faraway loved ones, can keep that touch light and impersonal. We say "let's have lunch soon" over and over, month after month, into a piece of beige plastic, but we may never actually get around to it.

Then there are cars, little living rooms on wheels that restrict what could be a meaningful friendship to a series of perfunctory waves, as day after day the garage doors spit us out into a world across town.

Our cars may even be carrying us to church, which is often just a larger cocoon with pews! How ironic that the perfect community center should seal us off from our communities. How sad that "Christian activities" should keep us from such an important Christian activity: loving our neighbors.

But why not use these twentieth-century conveniences to *keep* the Tenth Commandment rather than break it?

Your minivan can become the Sunday Express for the kids of friends who would probably let them go to church with you (if for no other reason than to have a quiet Sunday morning at home).

Your television can be the one-eyed host of next week's NFL-game party. Why not invite those old friends who've been on your heart anyway?

Your living room can become a haven for your neighbors whose daughter ran away, or who just lost a job. If they know you care, the smell of coffee from *your* kitchen window will be incense to them.

Sit Down to Stand Up

Coffee brings up the keeping of yet another commandment. You see, there's one low-tech item you already own that could be the key to seeing many people eventually come to Christ. In centuries past it has served as a valuable tool in planting thousands of churches, and in some cases has been the starting point of national revivals. What is this amazing invention?

In a phrase, your dining room table. In a word, FOOD! Remember the old saying that the way to a man's heart is through his stomach? Well, whoever said that may have known nothing about surgery, but he or she sure knew a lot about spiritual anatomy.

Jesus called himself "the bread of life" (John 6:48). Ephesians 5:18 likens the Holy Spirit to wine.

Jesus inaugurated His church and celebrated the New Covenant with a meal, comparing His body and blood to bread and wine. The early church subsequently was established around the dinner table, and for a long time the worship services took place there, so much so that Paul eventually had to set some rules concerning the special nature of Holy Communion (see 1 Corinthians 11).

Jesus even compares our ongoing heart-to-heart fellowship with Him to having a meal with Him (Revelation 3:20; see also Song of Solomon 2:4).

Give a man something good to eat and you own his approval and unconditional trust, at least for the time being. Give him a case of food poisoning and he'll probably never come to your house or restaurant again.

Professionals know the truth of this. Even realtors suggest that home sellers put a touch of vanilla extract in a bowl and keep it in a warm oven. Why? It makes the house smell like fresh cookies to a prospective buyer, and everyone knows that cookies smell like "home."

Smart Christians also know the power of food. When the Rock of Gainesville church wanted to reach onto the University of Florida campus, they did it by hosting a dinner reception for the school's varsity baseball team. This was but one act of Christian love that made them attractive to the university's most attractive group, its athletes. Little wonder, then, that this congregation's average age consistently hovers in the low twenties.

Believe me, a great way to love your neighbor as yourself is to feed him from your table. And it's a great way to prime his heart for the love of God.

You'll also be moving your friends toward an encounter with Christ by accepting the invitation to *their* table. Either way, whether at your table or theirs, an ideal way to stand up for Christ with friends is to sit down for a meal with them.

Supply-Side Christianity

You needn't act alone either. There's great power in bringing your friends into situations where they're in the company of other Christians. I'm not particularly referring to home Bible studies or house church meetings—although these are fine, if not inevitable, invitations to make.

Rather, I'm talking about softball games, Super Bowl parties, Christmas programs, Labor Day picnics, any event that brings Christians together. Welcome your friends into your Christian world!

"Aw, I'm afraid some of my Christian friends would either be too spooky or too right-wing for them," you say. "They might really feel out of place."

Hey, let me tell you what they'll notice. They're going to hear believers discussing their kids, children whose school grades and behavior on the whole would be the envy of people all over town, were the facts better known. And even if we churchgoers can tend to be a little out of touch, we're still a happy lot when juxtaposed with today's cocktail crowd. By comparison, your friends are going to see contentedly married couples and hear social commentary that is based on a foundation of moral absolutes. And it may be the first party in a long time where they don't witness someone in need of a "designated driver" when it's time to go home.

Believe me, there's a compound effect to righteousness, a fellowship among Christians that we take for granted, yet is palpable to unbelievers.

How to Pray the Game

All that we've discussed here—listening, gift-giving, productive work habits, opening your home, sharing meals—all of it is designed to enrich the lives of your friends and neighbors, while establishing a relationship with them that practically and naturally displays your faith in Christ. In other words, such generosity is not an alternative to talking about your faith but is actually a part of it. It should be clear that you're doing these things from an overflowing heart, not from some artificial motivation; because God's love propels you to "love your neighbor as yourself."

This means talking about your faith as naturally as you discuss the menu in a restaurant. It means saying, "Hey, let's bless the food" and jumping right in with a smile rather than nervously asking permission.

And remember, a meal isn't the only occasion for prayer with friends. Almost any place or time is right, if you use wisdom.

Sometime ago while playing golf in southern California, one of my playing partners pulled a leg muscle about halfway through our four-hour round. We had been strangers when assigned to turn our pair of twosomes into a foursome, but we quickly established a rapport that made it easy to be out on the links together. Seeing that my new friend was in some pain, I tiptoed over to speak with him while someone else was teeing off.

"Look, if it's okay with you, I'm just going to quietly pray for you while we play the next couple of holes," I whispered. "Nothing loud or demonstrative, mind you. I'll just ask the Lord to touch you with His grace."

The man looked a little puzzled, but thanked me and limped on. A few minutes later I noticed him whispering to his wife in a rather animated way before walking over to me at another tee marker, a bright but still bewildered look on his face.

"What did you do?" he wanted to know. His leg was feeling fine.

"I just prayed," I answered with a smile. "After all, if God's all I crack Him up to be, He ought to be able to answer a little prayer like that, right?"

"Wow" was his next response, if I remember correctly. In any case, he thanked me again as we finished play on the last green, and then came over on the parking lot to express his gratitude one last time. It was there that I encouraged him to have his own conversations with the Lord, and to be open-hearted regarding the lordship of Jesus Christ.

Looking back now, the beauty of the event was that a relative stranger pursued me about the Lord for more than an hour, all because of one small act of kindness. How much easier should it be, then, as one Little League parent to another, to make the same offer on the sidelines? And what a perfectly natural gesture to follow up on it the next day by phone, or to simply wait until the next game rolls around.

Understand this: the proverbial man on the street doesn't mind at all when a Christian makes such an offer. In fact, he's usually pleasantly surprised, since we're so different from the mean-spirited caricature etched into his mind by biased news media and sacrilegious stand-up comics.

Be There *and* Be Square

From time to time, of course, your friends will find themselves ill-equipped to face the inevitable hardships that come to all of Adam's offspring. Whether they're dealing with minor depression or major illness, at such times you must be ready, without hesitation, to offer them a healing hand, not only the kind that is laid on the sick in faith but also the one that is simply there to hold on to.

Most people put aside their petty objections to Christianity and in fact become very religious in the midst of tragedy. Although every day is full of opportunities for demonstrating the life of Christ in you, these are especially important times to speak openly about Him, about the importance of full surrender to Him. Don't hold back. Don't try to be as subtle as you normally might. Now it's time to be there *and* be square, to be bold in your Christian presence.

Don't hesitate to offer to pray for your neighbor, right away, for God's comfort and presence. Then be ready to listen or simply to sit in silence with him. No matter what it costs, give him some measure of extra time, something more than your relationship demands.

Some of your friends will face bereavement. It's sad to say, but grieving people so often find themselves alone, as "friends" stop calling because they want the whole episode to be over. But it isn't over. On such a day, more than any other, you must be there. Be ready to talk as well as listen. Help your neighbor to mourn in God's way. As Richard Exley, my former pastor, paraphrases the words of Jesus in Matthew 5:4, "Blessed are those who let grief do its work, for they shall be healed."

There is also the probability that in some instances you will be a mourner, that you will outlive some of the old gang. And if you've been diligent to "love your neighbor as yourself," you'll probably get a call from one of them who knows he's staring at death.

Baseball greats Bobby Richardson and Mickey Mantle both played for the virtually invincible New York Yankee teams of the '50s and '60s. Richardson had witnessed about Christ to the fast-living, hard-drinking center fielder during those wonder years, but Mantle had ignored his soul in favor of his appetites. Nevertheless, Bobby wasn't deterred, and for more than thirty years he remained Mickey's friend, always reminding him that he was praying for him.

It wasn't until death was staring him in the face that the hobbled hero finally humbled himself before the Lord and committed what was left of his life to Jesus. Then, after praying, he immediately called Richardson to tell him. "I wanted you to be the first to know," said the dying man. Within the week, Mickey Mantle was with the Lord.

Bobby Richardson loved his neighbor.

For Thought and Discussion

1. Do you live a mostly "thou shalt *not*" life? Or is there an enthusiasm—a sense of relaxed, healthy freedom—that would cause your friends to ask, "Why *do* you enjoy life so much?" or "Why are you so free from cares and worries?"
2. Do you *care* about your friends and neighbors in a way they could actually *detect*? Or do you just feel guilty and pressured to "sell them" on your faith?

3. How could you invite your friends and neighbors into your world? How could you take part in theirs? Is your social and/or family life so centered in church activities that you have little relaxed, meaningful contact with nonbelieving friends?

4. How could you be a *true* friend to a friend today?

In Your Face:
Taking a Stand With Pleasure Seekers and Dirty Jokers

It was time to get a job. At twenty-three I had never held one outside the ministry. (No jokes, please.) Now, with four months between overseas journeys, I took a position selling cars in suburban Baltimore. The transition from missionary to car salesman had been anticipated by Jesus when He said, "I saw Satan fall like lightning from heaven." Evidently the Savior had personally witnessed Lucifer's descent into the auto trade.

My desk was out on the floor—the gates of hell, as it were—where we greeted those poor, misguided souls who had been suckered into our clutches by the shiny red and yellow machines on the front line. Even our products sounded devilish—like the Gremlin, named appropriately for a demon that causes mechanical problems, and the Javelin, a fast-moving instrument of death. We also sold Matadors—a Spanish "killer"—and Ambassadors, fiendishly named for that most diabolical character of all, the political appointee.

Well, maybe it wasn't quite that bad. The cars did come with the best warranty of their day, and the only horns were under their hoods rather than on management's foreheads. But being in the business had its netherworldly side nonetheless, like the time I said hello to the sixty-something woman who instantly whirled around and shouted, "Don't think you can pull that with me!" Then there was Lenny, a fellow sheetmetal monger and self-proclaimed Satanist, who brought a prostitute to work.

Lenny wanted to be the hippest, most hedonistic guy around. And if he couldn't *be* that guy, he at least wanted us to think he was. So he bragged. He bragged about cheating customers, about belonging to a local witches' coven, about picking up a girl in a bar one night and having sex with her in one of the new cars on the lot. And he positively gloated when he brought the gray-skinned, platinum-haired, bleary-eyed hooker into the showroom one morning.

Most of the guys were suitably impressed, flabbergasted, or mildly put-off—any reaction was okay with Lenny. Except mine. I wasn't shocked, or even offended, for that matter. Instead I felt sad, like when you read about some tragedy in the newspaper and can't do anything about it. I walked on over to my desk, offering him only a normal "Hello."

The warlock was piqued. He had to get at least a *little* rise from "the preacher." I heard him snicker and saw the woman coming toward me as I settled in at my desk.

"Are you a swinger?" she asked with a tone that said she had been dared to do it. "Lenny says you swing. Is that right?" Make-up was caked on her rugged complexion. She looked tired, and more "used" than any car on the lot, as though she'd been called "trash" often enough to believe it.

"No," I answered politely and without hesitation. "I'd rather be happy by being faithful to the wife God gave me. I'm not interested in any other way of living."

She apparently wasn't accustomed to multisentence conversations. Assignment over, she sauntered back toward Lenny, whose eyes met mine. A blush mushroomed across his face, as though a tiny A-bomb had detonated somewhere inside him. He had tried so hard to look cool but ended up looking silly. His ringmaster persona had given way to the sad clown he really was.

He never tried to take me on again.

The Company of Sinners

I could have responded differently, of course. I could have said a nervous "no" and turned away in hopes that the she-devil would disappear. I could have stiffened and said, "I'm a Christian, and you two should be ashamed of yourselves." I could have told them both to take a hike, or just glared at them without saying a word.

Since Lenny was involved in witchcraft, I could have interpreted the whole episode in terms of spiritual warfare, using the Lord's name a lot in my response, while doing some serious "authority-taking" under my breath.

I could have even gotten Lenny fired. Big Joe, the owner, would not have been amused to learn that this little farce had been played out in his showroom on company time. In fact, as a Christian concerned for his employer's well-being, maybe I *should* have reported the guy. But I didn't.

Any one of those responses would have shown weakness on my part, which was precisely what Lenny wanted to see. It would have shown him a Christian who wasn't strong enough to keep company with sinners.

I didn't want to give him the satisfaction, not so much because of personal pride—hey, who cared—but because I couldn't stand seeing another Christian get ground into the carpet. (This was 1973, the year that the United States Supreme Court cleared the way for the slaughter of millions of babies, and thus the year that millions of believers woke up to learn how irrelevant and ineffective we were.)

Instead I decided to show the company pagan, as well as the few semi-pagans who rounded out our sales crew, at least one Christian man who was no easily embarrassed starched shirt. I wanted them to see, after all of the boozing and boasting about real and alleged marathons of immorality, who it was that went home with a clear conscience every night and came to work with clear eyes every morning.

Why get Lenny fired? The guy needed to keep his job long enough to rub elbows and, when necessary, cross swords with a happy—though highly imperfect—Christian man. And skirmishes like this one provided a clear contrast for the other men too. The Romans in the stands need to see a lion lose once in a while, but that can't happen if the Christians down in the arena think their only choices are running away or lying down. I decided to do neither, opting instead to let the beast break his fangs on my armor.

> Therefore put on the full armor of God, so that when the day of evil comes, you may be able to stand your ground, and after you have done everything, to stand. Stand firm then, with the belt of truth buckled around your waist, with the breastplate of righteousness in place, and with your feet fitted with the readiness that comes from the gospel of peace. In addition to all this, take up the shield of faith, with which you can extinguish all the flaming arrows of the evil one. Take the helmet of salvation and the sword of the Spirit, which is the word of God. And pray in the Spirit on all occasions with all kinds of prayers and requests (Ephesians 6:13–18).

I was clothed with truth, righteousness, the gospel of peace, faith, and salvation, and armed with the Word of God. Why give an inch? Why pout or run for cover when you're wearing God's armor and carrying His sword? To the contrary, when you've "put on Christ" (Romans 13:14, cf. Galatians 3:27), you look just like Him in the eyes of the enemy! And he shudders at the sight.

Fans of spiritual-warfare teaching, take note: Yes, we wrestle against "principalities and powers" and rulers of darkness, *but who said the fight was such a close one*? Take a break from the battle now and then and go have lunch with a sinner!

The Friend of Sinners

While Jesus was having dinner at Levi's house, many
tax collectors and "sinners" were eating with him and
his disciples, for there were many who followed him.
When the teachers of the law who were Pharisees saw
him eating with the "sinners" and tax collectors, they
asked his disciples: "Why does he eat with tax collectors and 'sinners'?" On hearing this, Jesus said to them,
"It is not the healthy who need a doctor, but the sick. I
have not come to call the righteous, but sinners" (Mark
2:15–17).

Jesus dined with so-called sinners, like the tax collectors,
Levi (*aka* Matthew) and Zaccheus—while the real transgres-
sors, the religious critics who would eventually crucify Him,
stood around scoffing. Why was He so unruffled? Because He
knew the opposition was hopelessly overmatched.

You prepare a table before me in the presence of my enemies (Psalm 23:5).

The LORD will extend your mighty scepter from Zion;
you will rule in the midst of your enemies (Psalm
110:2).

He wasn't worried about being seen with the Lennys and
the Levis. Since He ruled in the midst of His pharisaical enemies, He could relax and have dinner among them too.

Jesus knew how to be a friend to sinners without sinning,
how to tame party animals without killing the party. His first
miracle was to produce fine wine for a wedding reception in
Cana (John 2:1–10). Whether it was real wine or remarkably
upscale grape juice, the other guests nonetheless hailed it as
a major enhancement to their celebration. They weren't used
to such quality so late in the festivities. In fact, they were accustomed to going from rich and fruity to cheap and watery as
the revelry wound down and their taste buds deadened.

The serving of wine, it seems, was a picture of human living. Thus Jesus, being the Redeemer, filled their cups with the best *after* they had exhausted their worst, just as He continues to do for empty souls today. And the contrast between the usual fare and what He offers, from Cana to car lot, is remarkable.

"But what about that verse that talks about light not having fellowship with darkness?" you say. Let's see exactly what the Scriptures say.

> Do not be yoked together with unbelievers. For what do righteousness and wickedness have in common? Or what fellowship can light have with darkness? What harmony is there between Christ and Belial? What does a believer have in common with an unbeliever? What agreement is there between the temple of God and idols? For we are the temple of the living God (2 Corinthians 6:14–16).

Your question is answered in the first sentence: "Do not be yoked together with unbelievers." This is not a passage about sharing your friendship but about *joining* yourself. It specifically bars Christians, for example, from marrying unbelievers, or making other types of *covenantal* agreements with them. Jesus often ate in the homes of sinners, but He never promoted joint ownership with them. Why? Because such arrangements are the marks of shared character, mutual seals of moral approval.

Paul had already drawn the distinction for the Corinthians in an earlier letter.

> I have written you in my letter not to associate with sexually immoral people—not at all meaning the people of this world who are immoral, or the greedy and swindlers, or idolaters. In that case you would have to leave this world. But now I am writing you that you must not associate with anyone who calls himself a brother but is sexually immoral or greedy, an idolater or a slan-

derer, a drunkard or a swindler. With such a man do not even eat (1 Corinthians 5:9–11).

There's the key. The person to avoid is the so-called Christian "brother" who is unrepentant in his sin. Don't sit in the pew with him. Don't go to hear him preach. Don't even have a drive-through hamburger with him, until he has accepted the discipline of the church.

But as for sinners who don't pretend to be otherwise, try to find a table with a nice view!

Coming to Their Senses

I told you Lenny was enthusiastically "hedonistic." Hedonists are abject pleasure seekers, persons whose lives revolve around satisfying their senses. No matter what their station in life, rich or poor, they sate themselves on the spirits at hand. Examples abound.

Whereas a pig might gorge himself on silage and wallow around in his own muddy manure, the Hollywood hedonist pays dearly for sugar-free silage and claims the manure is good for his tan. Hedonists like Lenny, on the other hand, are unpretentious in their piggishness. Life means "use and be used," and don't bother relabeling lust as love.

Then there's run-of-the-mill Appetite Al, the guy who thinks it's normal to guzzle ten beers during a nine-inning baseball game, who can be found clutching his shotgun in a duck blind every Saturday before sunrise, but can't wake up for Sunday service.

It's pretty easy to find yourself heading for an early lunch when some foul-mouthed pleasure jockey starts prattling on about this purchase or that conquest, or tells a joke that assumes you share his low opinion of women. At such times it's tempting to decide that standing up for Christ includes permission to deck the guy.

But it is possible, believe it or not, to "bless those that nauseate you." (Okay, so I paraphrased!) *The key is in looking past the pig to find the man.* Remember, every one of us was created in God's image. And for reasons known only to himself, the Creator has chosen to let shadowy stamps of that image remain in men, flickering hints of the Christians He may yet raise to life from this bone pile called humanity. And remember, Jesus came "to seek and to save what was lost" (Luke 19:10).

That's precisely how you should view the lecherous, boozy boor who, like a dog marking territory, wants to spray his offensive scent on everyone around him: with an eye to seek and to save. Look for the trace of God's image, the potential strength in all that glaring weakness. Find the one aspect of his personality that may reflect the grace of God already at work in him.

He might be a prisoner of his passions, but such people frequently are also capable of great *compassion*. Lenny was brazen and cynical. But cynics, while they distrust everyone including themselves, are often *honest* about how jaded they are. Or he may be a wheeler-dealer. But they sometimes turn out to be great leaders.

This is more than just a cute suggestion about turning lemons into lemonade. I'm telling you that God's amazing grace not only can "save a wretch like" the one at work, but that He's already planted the seeds of redemption in that wretch's personality! You need to find and feed and water them like crazy.

Shamelessly Righteous

In the long run, pleasure addicts—all of them—are only seeking God anyway.

- The Samaritan woman at the well (John 4) was seeking true intimacy, but looking in the wrong embrace. Jesus taught her to worship God.
- Alcoholics are thirsty for God's Holy Spirit, as Ephesians 5:18 infers, but they're drinking from the wrong bottle.

- Jesus kept company with gluttonous sinners because He knew they were hungry for the true Bread of Life (John 6:35).

Every man—from Samaritan to swinger—hungers for the fruit of the Spirit. And when he sees it, whether he's willing to admit it or not, he craves it. That's why Lenny kept testing me, because he was trying to find out if the "real thing" had shown up on the doorstep of his polyester world. I just happened to see him coming and decided to be shamelessly righteous!

Humility doesn't have to be—*shouldn't* be—shy. Back-at-you boldness is a virtue when it's garnished with the Spirit's fruit. Nowhere was that ever clearer to me than in the former Soviet Union.

Dolly and I had just finished a seven-city, twenty-five-day, tension-filled tour. Now it was time to board the ferry from Estonia, back to Finland's freedom. But this time we weren't traveling alone. Also aboard was Marju Kuut, one of the USSR's most popular singers and a recent convert to Christianity. She and her teenage son, Uku, were being forced to do what so many of their fellow citizens dreamed of doing: leave the Soviet Union.

The changes in Marju's life had been plentiful, sudden, and dramatic. When the pop star had committed her life to Christ she was an alcoholic whose every day started with vodka for breakfast. Now the perpetually puffy eyes were clear, the leathery look gone from her detoxified skin. For years her every sentence had brimmed with vulgarity. Now her concerts were filled with thanks to God for saving her.

The fact that Soviet news agencies routinely suppressed such stories had served to create a national rumor mill that was a model of efficiency, perhaps the only smooth-running and reliable machine Marxism ever produced. The whole country was abuzz with rumors about Marju's faith and the obvious transformation that had accompanied it. To the authorities this meant the immensely popular singer had to go, either to prison or to the West. It was easier and less messy to kick her out of the country.

Now, as she sailed toward unknown freedom, the raven-haired ex-Soviet recounted her remarkable journey to faith in God, a journey that had begun two years earlier with a concert that was not her own.

Living Sound, the ministry we served, had grown into four sets of "musicianaries," traveling to all corners of the earth with the Gospel. That year the newest, youngest team had taken the wheel of our used touring coach in England and headed for the Soviet Union, tourist visas in hand. We had left the original owner's defunct company name and logo on the side of the bus, and apart from a ton of guitars and loudspeakers in the luggage bins, they appeared to be just another group of harmless Westerners in the mood for the worst vacation of their lives.

The team arrived in the Estonian capital of Tallinn, and checked into the only hotel officially designated for *Amerikanskis*. Now it was time for supper downstairs in the only officially designated *restoran*—which quickly proved to be an establishment with very bad cooks in the kitchen and a very good singer onstage. Marju was in concert.

During a break between sets our rookie team swung into action. A couple of our own band members walked around to the side of the stage and looked at the antiquated instruments the Soviet musicians had played. "Band," said one of the guys. "Drums . . . guitar," he continued, pointing to his partner and himself. "Rock and roll!"

He sounded like Tarzan reading a see-and-speak picture book, but his point was made. Immediately the wide-eyed Estonians vacated the stage, and the young American Christians were making their Evil Empire debut. By midnight the Tallinn rumor mill was in gear, and the whole city knew that foreigners were singing about God in the Viru Hotel.

"They were very good players," Marju told me. "But it

wasn't so much the concert or the lyrics that impressed me. Instead it was how the group acted offstage.

"In the first place they didn't have to get drunk in order to perform. And they were so nice to one another! The men were polite to the women, holding doors for them and helping them to the table. And the ladies were also very kind. They even helped the band with their gear."

Marju spent every waking moment with the team from that night on, listening to them talk, watching them perform, going to church with them—a dangerous career move—and watching them get hauled in for KGB "interviews." She knew her own grilling would follow as soon as the group left the country. But she was so taken with their habit of giving thanks "in all things" that she had to stay with them, had to learn more.

Soon she made the decision to serve God, no matter what the future might hold. Another lion(ess) had been tamed, another principality foiled. But not because of moving songs or persuasive sermons. The American visitors had plenty of both, mind you. But their real power, the same power that's yours to wield in the face of brandied breath and jaded comments, was their unbridled goodness. They were shamelessly righteous.

Putting a Lid On It

Once in a while there's simply no alternative. Sometimes standing up for Christ leaves you no choice but to stop the trash-talker in his tracks, to stomp the serpent's head even if it means breaking someone's toes in the process.

But most Christian men aren't confident in their ability to obey Paul's instructions on either *how* or *when* to exhibit righteous indignation.

> Therefore each of you must put off falsehood and speak truthfully to his neighbor, for we are all members of one body. "In your anger do not sin": Do not let the sun go

down while you are still angry, and do not give the
devil a foothold (Ephesians 4:25–27).

Gets harder as it goes, doesn't it? Don't lie; no problem. Tell
the truth to my neighbor; well, sometimes I'd sooner let things
pass. But be angry without sinning? Hah! (Try doing my taxes
sometime!)

Anger needn't be a launching pad for resentment. It's important to understand that "righteous anger" is righteous because it's based on a righteous standard: the Bible. When
God's Word draws a line in the sand, you remain in safe territory when somebody crosses it. Expressing righteous anger—like spanking a child or punishing a criminal—comes
with certain rules.

- It is never to be exercised on nonscriptural grounds.
- It is never to be withheld on nonscriptural grounds.

So when is it appropriate to be angry? Generally such a
time comes when . . .

- Repentance appears to be out of the question.
- Silence would indicate your approval of a repulsive statement or action.

Dolly and I once found ourselves in precisely that situation
during a tour of South Africa, where I was ministering primarily in white churches, challenging them to not merely express sorrow for past racism, but to embrace their black brothers while time remained.

One evening at dinner with our hosts, we found ourselves
joined by their unbelieving brother who was in town for the
night. We enjoyed a feast of fresh mussels and pasta before re-
tiring to the sitting room for conversation. As usual the topic
of *apartheid* came up. South Africa wasn't America. Things
were different there. Still, there was no excuse for discrimi-
nation anywhere. It was the kind of conversation where you
hope your views are about the same, but you don't assume
anything.

The brother was quiet at first, but after a third or fourth glass of wine, he joined right in. "Our blacks are different from your blacks." Talking about people as though they were possessions made me tighten a little. Dolly squeezed my hand and winked, as if to say, "Don't worry; we're going home in an hour."

"I don't allow my garden boy to shake a white woman's hand. If he shakes her hand today, he thinks he can sleep with her tonight." Our host, a dedicated Christian man who wanted to win his brother, tried to intervene. It didn't work.

"I'll tell you what should have happened. Hitler should've started in the Cape and worked his way north. . . ."

Suddenly I was off the couch and in the air. "No more!" I shouted. "Enough! I flew five thousand miles on donated funds in order to come here and preach the name of Jesus, not reminisce about Hitler."

"Ach, forgive me if I offended—"

"Don't apologize to me. Repent! You don't offend me; you sicken me! It's twenty-eight million black people to whom you should apologize." I headed for the door. My collar was on fire.

He walked to the door and extended his hand. I kept mine lowered, stared him in the face, and lowered my tone as well. "I'll not shake your hand. I'll shake hands with your 'boy,' but I won't shake yours."

We thanked our mortified hosts for dinner, bade them goodbye, and walked out into the cool African breeze. And somewhere deep in my pounding heart, I heard a small voice say, "Good job, son."

Wisdom's Fruit

Silence can be every bit as effective as the most brilliantly crafted speech. Jesus gave "resounding" proof of this when He stood before Pilate and His Jewish accusers. Matthew recalls that the Savior "made no reply" (Matthew 27:12–14). Why not? After all, He was the "Word made flesh." He had both the ability and the right not only to answer them, but to roundly, eloquently condemn them.

Most folks have been led to believe that Jesus muted himself because He lived somewhere on a higher plane, possessing a sort of "mother of the year" love and patience. They've been taught to see His death as a supreme act of love, by a God willing "just this once" to grant universal amnesty to mass murderers, tax cheats and cookie-jar thieves alike. Neato! Now Jack the Ripper and Dennis the Menace can *both* go to heaven!

That's not why He did it. Jesus' passage down the *Via Dolorosa* was more than the ultimate sentimental journey. While history's greatest love was indeed poured out that day, it was justice that prescribed each step.

Earlier Jesus had said "wisdom is proved right by her actions" (Matthew 11:19), meaning that the wisdom of His deeds could be seen in the fruit they produced. In this instance, to answer His accusers would have been to justify this outrageous kangaroo court. But in reality God had convened these proceedings for the purpose of indicting the indictors, whose guilt was being established beyond all doubt or excuse by their own ricocheting charges. Thus "God's secret wisdom, a wisdom that has been hidden and that God destined for our glory before time began" (1 Corinthians 2:7) called for quiet. It was a tactic. *Holding His peace was a response, not a lack of one.*

That's what gives silence its "golden" reputation. Sometimes staying quiet gives the loudmouth time to snare himself. It's like giving a fish more line in order to tire him out. Eventually he surrenders.

Years ago a Korean radio interviewer tried to lay a trap by asking me a politically loaded question during a time of national unrest. I was starting to panic until the Holy Spirit inspired just the right response. Smiling at my host, I simply closed my mouth, miming a zipper motion across my lips. Then I sat there, letting dead air kill his show, entertained by the spectacle of an attacker surprised to find his own grenade tossed back at him.

This is what happens to lout and lecher alike. Given enough time they defeat themselves. That's why the term "party animal" is ironically accurate. Animalistic people, like animals, tend toward self-destructive behavior. They're really not that hard to trap.

Invariably the dirty joker will go too far even for himself. Dennis was another car salesman during my brief career in chrome. Not quite the swinging Satanist, he nonetheless regularly exhausted his vocabulary of vice in trying to find my limits. And when he ran out of regulation curse words, he would invent new ones—adverbs, verbs, adjectives, and nouns, all strung together in phrases like "bleeper-bleeping bleepers who bleeping bleep the other bleepers."

One day Dennis resorted to a particularly low bleep about Christians, actually managing to violate his own subterranean standards. I wondered how he would talk himself back to the surface.

"Hey, don't get me wrong. I believe in God!"

Opportunity knocked on the monastery door. My vow of silence was about to end with a big *Gotcha!*

"Wow!" I said in mock wonder. "Dennis believes in God! Boy, I'll bet that makes poor old God's day. He's probably been sitting around waiting, neglected for months, hoping big, manly Dennis might say a word in His favor again this year. Oh, now it's been worth it all! God can go back to sleep."

It was one little paragraph, but it blasted the mouth that roared into verbal oblivion. Dennis practically crawled under his desk. The Baron of Bilge was finished, his lips shuttered like an abandoned tenement. And from that day forward a respect for God was established on the showroom floor.

Let Wisdom teach you the difference between the "time to keep silent and [the] time to speak" (Ecclesiastes 3:7). Each is a proper response in its setting, and wise sequencing of the two will lead eventually to the dirty talker's:

(a) conversion

(b) outright hatred or ridicule (sure signs of progress)

(c) permanent self-censorship in your presence, a sign that you've established respect for Christ's name with that person, even if he isn't converted.

Shortly before I left the company to resume my normal tours of duty, I got a phone call one evening. The man on the other end of the line was devastated. His wife was having an affair and wanted a divorce. He couldn't live without her. He would change; he would do anything to keep her and save his marriage. He needed God to have mercy and help him. Would I please pray with him right then?

It was Lenny.

For Thought and Discussion

1. Who are the guys in your life who always seem to have the most corrupt stories, jokes, and attitudes? Do you avoid them? Tune them out? Tell other people how disgusted they make you feel? Lecture them?
2. How could you show genuine concern for these guys?
3. How could you demonstrate a kind of friendship that overlooks their behavior?

7

If There's a God, Then Why. . . ?
Taking a Stand with Skeptics and Cynics

I remember the Spanish *Costa del Sol* of seventeen summers ago as a vacation brochure come to life, a necklace of red-roofed, white-washed villages and villas draped around the blue Mediterranean's sunny shoulders. I remember eating *paella* on the tiny Valencian islet where it originated. And I vaguely remember that the rain in Spain fell mainly on Madrid.

And there are other memories that remain vivid. Like the time we did a lunch-hour university concert in Alicante. Or tried to. Actually we spent most of the first few songs dodging paper planes and attempting to be heard above the din of a student-communist audience intent on booing us *yanquí imperialistas* back to America. In a few weeks post-dictatorial Spain would go to the polls to choose between socialism and parliamentary democracy—and this crowd clearly didn't want any capitalists, Americans, or Christians around to muddy up the works. Thus they despised us threefold, and I think threw triple the paper for emphasis.

Barely ten minutes into the fray I decided it was time to either give up or speak up. Since nothing harder than airborne origami had hit me, I chose the latter and stepped to the microphone.

"One thing I know about you socialists," I said, wading right in. "You hate insincerity and hypocrisy. But you value honesty."

They were trapped already. The capitalist pig had simultaneously complimented and challenged their leftist sense of honor.

"Well, we could stand here and sing nice, vague songs about peace and love and brotherhood without ever mentioning Jesus, but we would be liars and hypocrites. Maybe you're right and we're wrong, but we believe He *is* peace, He *is* love, and that true brotherhood is impossible without Him. So we have no choice but to sing about Him.

"However, we're not going to try to prove our claims about Jesus, because we believe He can and will reveal himself as the Savior of the world to any truly open-hearted person.

"You don't have to listen to us. But we have to be honest, because you socialists demand honesty, and we respect this demand. All we ask is your respect in return. So if you're going to stay, then stop making noise."

No one left. The Holy Spirit had inspired serpentine wisdom combined with dovish innocence (Matthew 10:16). To leave would have been an admission of close-mindedness, as much a mortal sin for Spanish socialists as for American liberals. They *had* to remain.

Paper missiles were hangared back in notebooks, and heckling gave way to applause. When we finally ended our last song and descended the stage, each of us was immediately surrounded by eager questioners. The students wanted to hear more about Jesus Christ and how to know Him. We talked and prayed with them into the afternoon.

The Church grew that day.

Détente With the Devil

Of course, you're not likely to face a band of communists who want to throw you out of their country. But maybe you've encountered your share of angry feminists, anti-Christian environmentalists, and militant homosexuals—not to mention burned-out, backslidden believers—who wanted to silence you right here at home. You don't mind being labeled "right-wing." That's inevitable, and it puts you in pretty good company these days anyway. But how do you stand up for Christ in a *positive* way with these people? Or do you just settle for a truce? Is such a truce possible, or even permissible?

You may be facing required, but perverse, "sensitivity training" at work, or dealing with your child's New Age schoolteacher. Saying nothing amounts to surrender; you know that already. But how can you act *redemptively* in the situation? Maybe you'd just like to be able to answer the office atheist when he starts in on how ridiculous it is to believe in a Creator. But how can a Christian who never finished college rebut someone who sounds like he memorized the *Humanist Manifesto* as a child?

Well, I'm happy to tell you it really isn't that hard to survive, even thrive, in situations like these. In fact, I'll let you in on some secrets to success right up front.

First, don't worry. Skeptics and cynics and self-proclaimed enemies of Christ may rail and roar, but they don't worry God, so they shouldn't worry you. As the late Christian apologist Paul Little once said, "It is improbable that anyone thought up, last week, the question that will bring Christianity crashing down."

Second, don't think you have to achieve some sort of détente with the devil. Remember what we said in Chapter 3 about the true balance of power that exists between you and anyone needing Christ. *In every situation, at all times, you have the advantage.* While you may have to "agree to disagree" for a period of time, remember that the Holy Spirit isn't called the Hound of Heaven for nothing. He is at work in the conscience of the unbeliever, either convicting him of the truth of sin and judgment (John 16:8) or giving him over to a depraved mind (Romans 1:28), so that he will be without excuse when he faces final judgment.

Third, realize that this person's prejudice against Christ in you—and this is *always* the case—springs more from personal dissatisfaction than careful study. His views on Christianity and Christians are probably knee-jerk reactions, and even if he's full of statistics and so-called facts, they were most likely compiled for the sake of justifying resentment formed long ago from inward hurt.

Fourth, understand—and then counter—the mindset that defines Christians as nothing more than narrow-minded people who are against a lot of things.

Think about it. What are modern Christians best known for? The answers should be easy. In the eyes of the public, we're against abortion, pornography, and euthanasia (and rightly so). Of course, on every issue we also claim to be *for* what is right. For example, we're pro-life and pro-family, but when pressed to define those terms, we often end up in the "anti" column again. Pro-life doesn't really mean pro-baby— our low birth and adoption rates prove that. No, in terms of actual practice, it simply means that we are anti-abortion. And "pro-family" gets tossed around in such vague terms that even homosexual couples try to claim it as their own. *True righteousness remains undefined, to our detriment.*

Your response to this twisted picture must be to untwist it, to let this disillusioned person see a Christian who promotes what's good rather than just protesting what's wrong. You may already be doing this to some extent, giving witness to a happy marriage in the face of sexual perversity, for example. But countering the image of Christians as bespectacled prigs in collective need of a liberal Heimlich Maneuver is going to require *overtly* righteous behavior, somewhat similar to the "shamelessly righteous" conduct we recommended earlier.

Thus you should be as joyful as your foes are strident. Feel free to offset their stands by exhaling the simple, daily goodness of life in Christ. Don't keep God's blessing a secret.

Finally, establish your honesty with the opponent of your

faith, so he understands that even if you're wrong, at least you hold your convictions honorably. Doing this personalizes any future outbursts against Christian beliefs and morals. He won't be able to rail against "those people" anymore without attacking you, and that will probably cause him to weigh his words more carefully.

The People vs. Jesus Christ

> But even if you should suffer for righteousness' sake, you are blessed. "And do not be afraid of their threats, nor be troubled. But sanctify the Lord God in your hearts, and always be ready to give a defense to everyone who asks you a reason for the hope that is in you, with meekness and fear; having a good conscience, that when they defame you as evildoers, those who revile your good conduct in Christ may be ashamed. For it is better, if it is the will of God, to suffer for doing good than for doing evil (1 Peter 3:14–17, NKJV).

When it comes to dealing with skeptics, Peter really says it all in a few verses. First he claims that a little rejection never hurt anybody, that suffering "for what is right" is a blessing, an honor. Most people think that's the Bible's typological way of kissing a believer's "boo-boo" to make it all better. But read it again. Suffering for righteousness' sake is a *blessing* from God! Blessings are rewards, not consolation prizes.

This isn't a matter of pretending horrible medicine tastes good so your little brother will swallow it. Peter is telling the truth here. And need we be reminded that the apostle and his readers routinely faced suffering of a type more severe than our putting up with the prating of an irate feminist who just found out we voted conservative?

The old "but they won't like me anymore" fear isn't worth holding on to, if you ever had it. Maybe it made you take up smoking in the seventh grade, but it doesn't have to stunt your growth in taking a stand for Christ. Besides, where's the honor in being too worthless to throw to the lions?

Peter lets a prophet help him make his point. "Do not say, 'a conspiracy,' concerning all this people call a conspiracy, nor be afraid of their threats," he says, quoting Isaiah 8:12. In fact, he immediately quotes Isaiah's next verse also, although contemporary punctuation doesn't reflect it. But if you look at the Old Testament passage, you'll understand what he meant.

> Do not say, "A conspiracy," concerning all that this people call a conspiracy, nor be afraid of their threats, nor be troubled. The LORD of hosts, Him you shall hallow; Let Him be your fear, and let Him be your dread. He will be as a sanctuary, but a stone of stumbling and a rock of offense to both the houses of Israel, as a trap and a snare to the inhabitants of Jerusalem (Isaiah 8:12–14, NKJV).

Makes more sense, doesn't it? Peter is essentially saying, "If you're going to be awed by someone, let it be by God rather than your enemies."

Then he instructs us to "always be ready to give a defense" regarding our faith in Christ. Does this mean you've got to let people put you on trial for being a Christian? Or does giving a defense entitle you to fight back? Well, I've known one or two folks who used "defending the faith" as an excuse for meanness, but that's not what the Scripture is getting at. (Somehow people like that manage to offend more than defend anyway.)

Peter is simply saying you should never turn down a request to discuss Jesus and explain why you serve Him. And he implies that a Christian's faith should be enough of an open book that someone will come around asking about it. Of course, this is a bit like chumming for sharks in today's world. All you have to do is dangle Jesus' name in a conversation or two and some people think they smell blood in the water.

This is precisely why the phrase "with meekness and fear"

sets the tone for the proper response. When some self-appointed Clarence Darrow protégé decides to put the average Christian man's belief in God on trial, the besieged brother's temptations run in two directions. One is to say, "I'd rather not argue about this"—which may be true, but is probably followed mentally by, "I'm afraid I might lose." The other, if the plaintiff is particularly obnoxious, is to tell him to go rejoin Darwin up in the trees until he "evolves" some manners.

Peter rules out both reactions. "Always . . . give a defense . . . with meekness and fear." This means you should neither run from a fight nor pick one. Instead you should humbly, truthfully, and in friendly tones if possible, explain why you follow Christ. Maybe you can't explain coelacanths and fossils and Einstein's hairdo, but so what? The pro-monkey crowd can't prove their side either. That's why Darwin's views are called *theories.*

So, doesn't this mean you're stalemated? No. Beyond all argument or discussion, just be a witness and tell what you know to be the truth. It's up to the guy that thinks he's an ape's nephew to decide whether he believes you.

Giving a defense of your faith doesn't mean engaging a debate, although a debate can be fruitful if you're prepared for it. And by "prepared" I don't mean doing your doctorate at Harvard and living with gorillas in Zaire. It's simpler than that. The Creation issue provides the perfect example, so let me stay with it a little longer.

Creation scientists, usually avowed believers in Jesus, very often make the elementary debating mistake of arguing their case on their opponents' terms.

The whole debate *presumes* that human beings have the ability to authoritatively comment on a transcendent God. Romans 9:20 shows that man has no right to speak *against* God. And we well-meaning Christians need to realize that man also has no ability to speak *for* God, outside of His Word and our personal witness. (See Revelation 12:11.)

Christians should not—in fact *cannot*—subject a transcendent God to a finite system of observation. "But it's *science*," someone says with dangerous reverence. "If we could just come up with *scientific* evidence of God's existence, it would be a great testimony." Would it? Is man *entitled* to empirical proof that Jesus lives before he's required to bow the knee? Does faith come by hearing Carl Sagan's acknowledgment that God put "billions and billions" of galaxies in place?

No, faith came because I heard God's Word (Romans 10:17), which had a supernatural effect in my heart (Hebrews 4:12, cf. Jeremiah 23:29), causing me to believe (Romans 10:9–10). God's truth is better spoken than argued. Why not rely on what David said? "The law of the LORD is perfect, reviving the soul. The statutes of the LORD are trustworthy, making wise the simple" (Psalm 19:7).

Debating a skeptic on his ground is pointless, even counterproductive. But God's perfect Word has power to convert the soul. So stick with what the Bible says. Explain humbly and meekly, assume the truth of Scripture, and leave the rest to the Holy Spirit.

Of course, you can't rely on Scripture you don't know. So it's wise to take our advice from Chapter 3 and prepare yourself before answering Goliath's taunts. While you needn't understand the finer points of quantum physics, you should be able to quote meaningful Scriptures accurately and without fumbling through the Bible trying to find Titus or Philemon.

After you've answered, if the skeptic still wants to argue with you, ask him if he's read the Bible for himself, actually *studied* it. Many attacks on Christians are by people just parroting what they've heard, rather than learning for themselves. Meet him right there at his point of weakness. If he hasn't studied what it means to have faith in Christ, then ask him politely why he presumes to dismiss yours. Suggest that he study the Scriptures seriously for a change, and offer to supply him with a decent study Bible. Then let the Holy Spirit do His work.

Oh, and don't be surprised if you still get slandered from

time to time. According to the Bible, if you've followed Peter's instructions your accusers won't be successful in making anyone other than themselves look bad. Besides, he says, if you're going to suffer, it's better "to suffer for doing good than for doing evil."

Do Atheists Exist?

Atheists are to the world of skeptics what pit bulls are to the world of dogs. If you're going to meet one, you want to be prepared. So let me tell you the first thing you need to know about atheists: *They don't exist.* Pit bulls exist, but atheists don't. There's no such thing as a man who believes there's no such thing as God.

Oh, there are plenty of people who *say* they don't believe in God. And there are lots more who believe in Him but hate Him. But according to the first chapter of Romans, there isn't a man on earth who truly, in his heart of hearts, believes in an accidental universe.

> For since the creation of the world God's invisible qualities—his eternal power and divine nature—have been clearly seen, being understood from what has been made, so that men are without excuse (Romans 1:20).

Without excuse. There's a phrase for the late twentieth century. Excuses are everywhere. Nothing is anybody's fault.

- A driver speeds off when she sees a police car. Pursued and caught with a million dollars worth of illegal drugs, she confesses that it was her twentieth such haul. But the evidence is dismissed by a judge who decides it was unreasonably obtained. Why? Because running from the police in a neighborhood like that is excusable. The woman goes free.

- An FBI agent is fired for gambling away two thousand dollars that he embezzled from the government. No fault of his, says the court, because his compulsion to gamble is a "handicap," and is thus federally protected. He wins reinstatement.[1]

- "Plead insanity," says the lawyer whose client murdered people and ate their remains. He knows he can hire a psychiatrist who'll say, "He's not responsible. He's sick. There's no other explanation for committing such a crime."

But there is an explanation, not only for unthinkable evils like cannibalism, but for the thinkable kind too, like idiotic court rulings. What is it? Well, I'll tell you right now it involves the most repulsive idea of our age. And it requires uttering the most politically incorrect word since the '50s. Send the kids out of the room. Here it is. The reason for evil in this world, and the reason *nobody* has an excuse is . . .

Sin.

Sin explains why people commit crimes and why judges let them get away with it. It explains why a killer kills, and why his victim dies. It explains why Adam ate the apple, why earthquakes happen, and why babies suffer. All of the evil in the world, in one way or another, is traceable to sin.

Atheists, deep down, understand this, as do their timid cousins, agnostics.[2] And they hate it. They don't want to face sin, theirs or anyone else's. But sin denied requires that evil be explained in other ways.

- The snake made me eat the apple.
- The woman you gave me—she's to blame.
- It was a *lack* of knowledge. . . . We had a right to that tree. . . . Religious repression is the real evil. . . . This stuff about God was just some rich businessman's excuse to control people and keep all the apples. . . . If I'm hungry and kill you, it's your fault for not letting me have some apples. . . . If there were a God, there would be enough apples. . . . The lack of apples is the root of all evil!

Okay, the rudiments of atheism may be a little more complicated than a fruit metaphor. But not by much. The basis for it is still a desire to escape accountability.

Atheists don't want to face God, but according to Scripture they clearly know He exists. When Psalm 14:1 says, "The fool says in his heart, 'There is no God,' " it isn't referring to some happy-go-lucky Forrest Gump who doesn't know any better. The term "fool" is applied here to one who self-consciously chooses depravity. In Hebrew it is derived from another word that means both *stupid* and *wicked*. The idea is that atheism is the sinner's utterly wicked, deliberately stupid choice to look God in the face and tell Him He isn't there. Atheists are spiritual *kamikazes.*

So how do you deal with a theological suicide bomber?

For starters, atheists almost always are people who pride themselves on logic, reason, scientific observation, and an appreciation for the lessons of human history. In other words, they set themselves up for defeat. How? Their entire faith— yes faith—*begins* by denying what their hearts know to be true, that God exists. Every contention that follows is based on that one. It's a little like arguing that Seattle is in England and then producing detailed maps to prove it. The maps don't matter if Seattle isn't there. Logic that starts with a lie isn't logical.

You, on the other hand, know that there is a Source of reason, that history is God's master plan, that Scripture is the ultimate form of logic, and—best of all—that the Holy Spirit convicts sinners. Thus you have the advantage. You don't have to prove anything. As Paul said,

> My message and my preaching were not with wise and persuasive words, but with a demonstration of the Spirit's power, so that your faith might not rest on men's wisdom, but on God's power (1 Corinthians 2:4–5).

I'm not implying that you have to reel off a few miracles to win the day. The "demonstration of the Spirit's power" is a reference to Paul's "message and [his] preaching." Whether miracles accompanied his sermons is beside the point. Here he is clearly talking about *words* with the power of the Holy

Spirit behind them. That's what you have. *The atheist has arguments, but you have God's supernaturally penetrating Word.*

He also has to rely on the history of man as his source of law. Right and wrong do not exist as absolutes, but rather as the accumulated lessons of humanity. If only enough of us will stop, look, and learn from the past, why, in no time at all we'll be on our way to establishing the Federation of Planets and putting down the Klingon Empire!

Putting On a Happy Face

Atheists these days are wont to call themselves "humanists," because it sounds pro-mankind as opposed to anti-God, and because it is reminiscent of humanitarianism, which celebrates human kindness. And to be fair, not all humanists would call themselves full-blown atheists. But in reality, the exaltation of man is always tantamount to the abasement of God. It's simply a one-seat throne.

My friend Al, both a humanist and a humanitarian, once asked me to watch a videotape produced by the American Humanist Association.[3] He wanted to know my opinion of it as a Christian. I agreed, provided I could pause the tape at any time to make comments.

In no time at all a hangman's noose was dangling before me. The film had promoted goodness without defining it. I hit the pause button.

"Al, would you say goodness ultimately must be defined by *consensus*—that it is what the majority of men mutually deem to be in the best interests of all concerned?"

"Yes, that's right."

"Okay, then let's reduce the world to five people: four men and a woman. Three of the men want to conceive children by the woman, in order to preserve the human race. But the woman wants nothing to do with them, and the fourth man agrees that this is her right. Therefore it's three to two. Three men, the majority, decide to rape the woman 'for the good of mankind.' And of course they have a point, since without children there eventually will be no mankind. Al, under these circumstances, can this woman's rape be defined as 'good' and 'right'?"

"Well, it's an unpleasant, strained example—but yes, I suppose in that case it could."

"Al, my dear Jewish friend, you have justified the Holocaust. Hitler persuaded a majority of his countrymen that mankind was better served by eradicating Jews. Only a brave minority believed he was wrong. And the only way you and I can also claim he was wrong is to admit that there must be an absolute standard of right. Without a higher authority, it's just our word against the Gestapo."

Al was shaken and said he wished there were more people present to discuss the subject. He really didn't want to talk any more. Sadly, I consented. But I'm waiting for another day, and in the meantime, counting on the Holy Spirit to reveal Christ in my kind friend's heart.

Al, if you're reading this, I love you.

Cynics

Skeptics, atheists, agnostics, humanists. You've probably noticed that these are sub-varieties of a single creature rather than separate species. They're all people who fear—for one reason or another, and to one degree or another—coming to God *on His terms*. And each one responds to that fear either by hijacking the apple tree or trying to hide among the figs. But whether aggressors or escapists, they all are Adam's sons.

You will encounter only one other nonreligious skeptic, and that is the *cynic*. He may or may not consider himself an atheist, agnostic, or humanist. He probably will scoff at such labels. In any case, there is one characteristic that earns him special mention here. Whereas the atheist wears his doubt like a badge, the cynic is garbed in pain.

Cynicism is skepticism with a heartache. Beyond the doubting of facts, a cynic doubts people. Just as an atheist is a frightened believer, a cynic is one who has suffered repeated injury to the soul. He's the one the Bible speaks about when it says, "Hope deferred makes the heart sick" (Proverbs 13:12). Whereas I never met a true atheist in the Soviet Union, I encountered an entire nation of cynics there.

Back in the "Evil Empire" days, every Soviet citizen, by his early teens, knew to awaken each morning prepared for the worst day of his life. Thus anything even remotely better could be classified as a nice surprise. Hoping for the slightest bright spot, however, would bring disappointment on any of a thousand days. The result was a generation of children with sullen spirits, where resentment could take root and grow, eventually afflicting every good thought, discoloring every decent idea, aborting every pleasant dream.

The whole nation was heartsick. No matter where you went, eyes like vacant, gray skies disclosed gloomy hearts that pulsed gray blood. Faces wore the blank pallor of sidewalks, and every word from every mouth seemed to carry Death's autograph.

It was in this suffocating atmosphere that my friend, Betsy, as part of a church-planting effort, started teaching English in Latvia shortly after the USSR had collapsed, freeing the tiny Baltic republic to become an independent nation once more.

One day Betsy asked her teenage students what careers they wanted to enter when they became adults. They just sat, looking puzzled, as though their American teacher had asked them to choose between window and aisle seats on a flight to Mars.

The instructor carefully rephrased her question. What did they want to achieve in life? Would they become doctors, writers, members of parliament, what?

"It doesn't matter," someone finally muttered, the others quickly nodding in agreement.

"Why doesn't it matter?" she asked.

"Because it will never happen. There's no point in dreaming about anything good, because it cannot possibly come to pass."

Betsy cried. Beneath the rubble of a thousand toppled statues of Lenin and Marx lay the dreams of these children and their parents before them. Three little words, "it doesn't matter," bespoke a half-century of sadness. There was so much more to teach here than English.

By the end of the school term, Betsy's students were learning a new language of the heart. Using a Bible as her textbook, she started teaching them how to hope in God. She realized now that she was a missionary in every way, that even a smile was instructive, and that laughter was no less than medicine (Proverbs 17:22). At this writing, several of her students are members of a thriving new church, one—I might add—that is particularly enthusiastic in praising God.

As Betsy's young charges demonstrated, cynics are easy to read and hard to touch. Their hurt comes through everywhere. They can neither give nor receive compliments or encouragement without resorting to some expression of sarcasm or despair. It usually takes more than a few gentle answers to turn away their wrath (Proverbs 15:1).

These folks are more hurt than angry. Their reactions tend to be automatic. Like a gag-reflex, their acid statements are a sign that something needs to come up. And therein lies the key to showing them Christ. Something does need to come up, and you need to help them get it out. The key is in recognizing the gift of God already at work within them.

Cynics frequently are very insightful people. They can accurately diagnose many of society's ills and are able to smell hypocrisy a mile away. *But their understanding of human nature has never been coupled with faith in God, which is why they've given up.*

You should keep your ears open for the truth these people often speak, and then nurture it by adding divine truth to it. Tell them you appreciate their insights as a gift from God.

Then ask if you can help them find answers to the problems they spot.

Most important of all, be patient. Keep your heart open to them, and wait for them to begin to reciprocate. It might be a while, but the payoff will be big when it finally comes.

High Tide

Water isn't necessarily the drink of choice for someone with a fully stocked wet bar or a refrigerator full of soft drinks. But to the man in the desert, withered from thirst, the most expensive champagne can't compare with a good mud puddle.

The naysayers we've described here are thirsty. Their rasping comes from dry souls. Real water is very satisfying to them once they find it. Or it finds them.

If you're facing a skeptic such as we've described in these pages, then the Living Water has found him. You're a portable oasis, a water truck, which God has driven into his spiritual Sahara. Your job is simply to overflow.

His opposition to you is really only the cursing of past disappointment, of having drunk sand from one too many mirages. His real enemy is no more flesh and blood than yours. In fact, you share a common foe whom Jesus decisively defeated long ago. Thus, though the doubter doesn't realize it, you're on his side.

When a skeptic of any stripe comes at you, you're under no pressure, no obligation to make him believe. You simply have the Water of Life, which the Holy Spirit will dispense at precisely the most tantalizing rate. So drip, pour, flow, or squirt; just don't turn off! Eventually God will either save the sinner or drown him.

Jesus sent the Holy Spirit to "convict the world of guilt in regard to sin and righteousness and judgment" (John 16:8). Believe me, He can do His job. Which means you can do yours.

For Thought and Discussion

1. Have you ever been drawn into a political debate about moral issues? Or a debate about evolution and creation? What was accomplished?
2. Can you explain in positive terms why you serve Christ— rather than arguing why you think your doctrine is right and others are wrong?
3. What meaningful scriptures could you suggest to a so-called atheist, skeptic, or cynic?
4. Are you comfortable, or uncomfortable, with the Bible's teaching that it is our *sin* that causes us to deny God's authority? If it came right down to it, could you challenge a skeptic to let go of his defensive unbelief and open himself to God just once to see what would happen? (Do *you* trust that God would act in some way to make himself known?)

Notes

1. Charles J. Sykes, *A Nation of Victims* (New York: St. Martin's Press, 1992), p. 3.
2. Agnostics essentially say that the existence of God can neither be proven nor disproven. Thus they are not sure that He exists, and will generally state that no one can be sure. The Latin word for agnostic is *ignoramus*.
3. Notable past members include the late science-fiction author, Isaac Asimov, and the equally late Gene Roddenberry, who created his own vision of the future and called it *Star Trek*. My earlier reference was intentional.

Casting Down Imaginations:
Taking a Stand With Pagans and Hypocrites

We had feasted on tropical fruit, exotic vegetables, and fine pastries, the best of everything, and still there was more food left over than our missions team had seen in our previous four weeks in Indonesia. Now our host was inviting us to sing, and Asian protocol required at least a mini-concert. Since our drums and guitars were under lock and key in the auditorium downtown, it fell to me to improvise a tune with the tools at hand.

Something was troubling me as I walked over to the old grand piano in the center of the sitting room. This Indonesian gentleman had led us to believe that he was a Christian, but there on the wall, beside a portrait of a very Western-looking Jesus, was an image of Confucius. And on the coffee table rested a crystal ball, along with an astrologer's chart. Other objects and images throughout the room clearly indicated that this was some sort of universalist meditation center, a spiritual ice cream parlor where Christianity was merely the religious flavor of the night.

The deception could not go uncountered, even at the risk of offending Asian hospitality. Otherwise we would leave thirty other guests with the impression that we too considered Jesus to be one god among many. I decided to make a pointed statement with a song that centered on Him as the only way to know God. The Savior's name landed like sparks on kindling. By the end of the piece, our host was showing signs of nervousness, his requisite smile thin and strained.

"Thank you, thank you for the lovely song," he intoned. "Of course, the important thing to remember is that we are all one. It really does not matter what we believe, as long as we are sincere." There it was—the drivel of false religion. I couldn't let it pass.

"What would you say if I told you that I disagree with you? That it *does* matter greatly what you believe, that you are 'sincerely' wrong, and that Jesus is the only way?" I softly retorted.

"I would say that you are correct, if that is what you truly believe," he said.

"So I am correct in saying you're wrong, and you are correct in saying you're right?" I asked, so as to make his commitment to absurdity clear to everyone.

"Yes. After all, we are all brothers, and that is the important thing."

Mike, our trombone player, stood to take the lead. "I'm sorry, but we are not brothers. We are not all one. Jesus is the only way. Thank you for your hospitality, but we cannot remain with you any longer. The time has come to say that we stand for Christ and Christ alone. We hope to see you at tomorrow's concert. You will be very welcome. Good-night."

The room was silent as we filed out the door, except for the soft humming of a man sitting lotus-like in an open window. Eyes closed, he was trying to escape the tension by chanting his way into a trance. It must not have worked too well. The next night, back at the auditorium, he came forward to commit his life to Christ and Christ alone.

Same Guy, Different Country

You've probably heard it from New Agers, schoolteachers, pop stars, Himalayan gurus, and pale little guys hawking candles at the airport. "It doesn't matter what you believe, as long as you're sincere." All over the world, that's the slogan of first resort for sinners wanting to create God in their own image.

The face and the language might be different, but you probably interact with this same person several times a day. Maybe you work with him, buy gas from him, even live next door to him. You certainly watch his movies and TV programs and read the newspapers he publishes.

Call him a New Ager. Call him a Hindu or a Buddhist. Call him the average American.

"Wait a minute," you protest. "I've read surveys that say the average American considers himself a born-again Christian." Sure he does. So did Mr. Sincerity in Indonesia. After all, why leave any gods out? Of course he wants to accept Jesus . . . too.

The guy down the block may not be as ditzy as some Hollywood starlet blathering on about reincarnation, or as weird as the maharishi who taught her. But ask him if he believes that any sincere person who has lived a good life will go to heaven, and he'll probably say yes.[1]

Purveyors of the "inclusion" doctrine pride themselves on viewing all religions as equal. It's a favorite, even sacred, tenet in any kind of setting where neutrality is required, which in today's culture means everywhere from Hollywood parties to political parties. It explains why guys running for office are always pointing wet fingers into the wind in order to find out what they believe, and why, once in office, they call on cocaine-snorting actors to give congressional testimony about the impact of industrial waste on our fragile ecosystem.

Of course, the sharp reader will remember that "neutrality," the sacred cow of secularism, is based on *exclusion*. Politics and education, for example, are supposed to be religiously neutral. Therefore religious principles, even minute religious references, must be excluded at all costs in the name of "preserving our precious freedoms." *Hmmm* . . . Oh, I get it! It's kind of like putting up a big wall in order to protect the people of East Berlin, right? Gee, what a neat idea.

Do you see where we're headed here? Suddenly the *inclusion* of all religions must be modified to *exclude* those that don't accommodate multiple paths to salvation. Therefore the tolerance of all points of view must be altered to tolerate *only* those views that agree with the tolerance of all points of view. So the only way to claim you've achieved total harmony is to silence those who disagree.

This is designer hypocrisy. More than the blind leading the blind, it is the blind passing laws against seeing.

Inclusion requires exclusion. Tolerance necessitates intolerance. Kinda reminds you of a shaggy little guru saying things like "God is everywhere and nowhere and everyone and no one and you are I and I am you and we together are one or perhaps nothing or definitely maybe everything or . . ." while adoring educators and artists sit around taking notes and wowing his profundity. (But what would they do if *he* answered 911?)

Absolutely No Absolutes

The New Ager usually says, "God goes by many names. There isn't any one right way. They're all right." Such a person looks at the absurd and sees divine mystery. He won't accept the divine mystery that God became a man and died on a cross. But he's willing to accept the illogical as a higher wisdom, because it is preferable to the simple truth that he is a sinner who needs to repent. Sin, and the cross, are too understandable, too threatening, too real. Absurdity offers him an escape from reason, and thus from the reality of his sin. It simply doesn't exist anymore.

Reality is totally redefined in the New Age consciousness

(which is preferable to having a New Age "mind" because it has more syllables). The grotesque is beautiful. Perversity is a right. Abortion is a choice, homosexuality an unchangeable genetic reality. All in all, this is Spin-Doctor Satan's ultimate twist on biblical faith.

"Now faith is being sure of what we hope for and certain of what we do not see" (Hebrews 11:1). Biblical faith is faith in God. New Age faith is less choosy. It's the substance of things wished upon a star, the evidence of things my psychic phone companion can see for $4.99 a minute. It is personalized pantheism, Hinduism with a California accent. And like the Golden State, it's riddled with fault lines just waiting to be shaken.

Crack number one is the New Age Absolute that there are no absolutes. "Everything is relative, that's for sure," says the great pretender, blissfully unaware of his contradiction. Unaware, that is, until you politely but purposely turn his cosmic credo in on itself.

"No absolutes, huh? Does that mean it's okay to kill the last whale in the ocean if we're really sincere?"

"No, of course not. Everybody knows that would be wrong," he'll protest.

"Well, maybe you're right," I come back. "But like they say about abortion—while I personally don't believe in killing whales, I don't think I have the right to force my opinion on Japanese trawler captains."

Your harmonically converged friend will likely become slightly detuned at this. His comeback will probably be something on the order of, "Don't be ridiculous. That's totally different."

To which you should reply, "What's different about it? Are whales more precious than developing babies? Can only their mothers and licensed whale abortionists kill them? Who grants them such license?

"Why can a woman choose to have her living, feeling, squirming fetus harpooned and suctioned out? Who says a schoolteacher is right to give a kid condoms, but wrong to give him a Bible? Tell me, on what basis are such decisions made? Who sets the standard?''

If at this point you're remembering our earlier suggestions about dealing with humanists and atheists, you're catching on quickly. The man who says God is everywhere is indeed the long-lost twin of the one who says He's nowhere. That's why the little guru can peddle his *all-gods-no-god* twaddle with such a straight face—he knows there's no real difference between the atheist and the pantheist. Both are essentially saying, ''I am God.''

No matter what the course of your conversations with New Agers, you will usually arrive fairly quickly at the all-important question of *who sets the standard*. In fact, it's inevitable, since their philosophy constantly assumes certain truths while denying Certain Truth. All you really need to do is let their own words take them back to this point again and again.

If your New Age friend starts getting angry, you've just rocked fault line number two in his philosophical landscape. Universalists universally resent the exclusivity of biblical Christianity, which is why they say lots of nice things about Jesus, but tend to carp about the Bible: ''It's outdated, too violent, too negative. Its origins are unreliable. It's full of mistakes . . .'' et cetera, on and on. Yessir, the proponents of all things warm and fuzzy emit some pretty negative vibes about the Book.

Here again they're welcome to fall victim to their own words, if not God's Word (Jeremiah 23:29). New Agers hardly ever are people who have read the Scriptures for themselves. Rather they've memorized verses and verse fragments, mostly out of context, sometimes out of thin air. You should take the opportunity to open the Bible as soon as your friend decides to bring it into the discussion.

As I've pointed out before, your main duty is to meekly and humbly give testimony to your faith in Christ (1 Peter 3:15), rather than to try to act as God's defense attorney. But you also have a responsibility to grow in your knowledge of God's Word, so you'll be ready for such golden opportunities.

Besides, you've got two things going for you. First, you probably are much more familiar with the Bible than your questioner. Second, there are Bibles with concordances, electronic Bibles, and all sorts of other tools available to compensate for your nonphotographic memory. Get one!

Now, I don't want to turn this into "Witnessing 101," but I would like to demonstrate how easy it is to deal with folks who try to quote a Bible they haven't actually studied. So arm yourself and romp with me through a little field of ignorance. Bullets mark the most common misquotes, and *italics* suggest responses. Don't bother to memorize them—just think on them awhile.

- The Bible says, "God is love." I think that means He accepts people of all religions.

Yes, 1 John 4:8 does say God is love. But look at the next verse, where it says that God's love was specifically shown to the world through His "one and only Son," Jesus. That word "only" points towards exclusivity, not away from it.

- I just don't think a loving God would send someone to hell if he tried to be the best person he could be. It wouldn't be fair. Besides, doesn't it say, "God is no respecter of persons"?

Yes, the apostle Peter said that in Acts 10:34, and followed up by saying that God proved His impartiality "in every nation" by sending His servants to preach "peace through Jesus Christ." In other words, the door is open to everyone, but there's only one door.

- Well, how do you know you're right and everyone else is wrong? After all, the Bible says, "judge not."

(Ah, the big one! "Judge not" is every New Ager's back-up mantra when "as long as you're sincere" starts failing.)

Right. Jesus himself said that in Matthew 7:1. But do you think He was actually promoting a lack of judgment? Should we send the Supreme Court home for good? Again, it's important to look at the rest of what He said. In the very next verse He made it clear that He was saying we can judge only if we're prepared to live and die by our own standards. In fact, in Leviticus 19:15 we're told to judge our neighbors fairly. Did you know that's where the founding fathers got the idea for our jury system?

The key is to gently argue (yes, argue) your New Age friend into the corner, and then humbly show him the way out. Of course, he may just turn off his mind to the truth, which is his religious impulse anyway. But the deception must be pointed out, whether in Indonesia or Indiana. He simply cannot have his cake and reincarnate it too. He has to make a choice.

You might make him angry, but that's okay. In fact, it's a sign of real progress to make a "universal peace and love" person angry by exposing his inconsistency. It's also sometimes necessary, in order to break the evil pride that is at the heart of New Age philosophy. Such is the price of *real* love, peace, and brotherhood.

And the Winner Is . . .

Many New Agers don't fit the New Age stereotype. They might even resent the label. To them, crystals are for chandeliers, trees are potential furniture, and pyramids are reminders of where they're headed on the corporate flow chart. I'm talking about success addicts, the people who are "doing just fine without your Jesus, thank you." Their religion is called *pragmatism*. It's a New Age sundae without the nuts, so to speak.

Their secular pastors hold forth on late-night television, exhorting viewers to awaken the Great Achiever within. Evidently three hundred bucks for a cassette series will rouse the giant. Toothy sermons of self-salvation are interwoven with testimonials from adoring disciples who joyfully report amazing personal growth, real-estate coups, new self-esteem, and no more waxy yellow build-up, all because they took the plunge and bought that course.

Demigods these, they speak to that part of a man that used to want a secret decoder ring, the part that still wishes there were a direct route to power, wealth, and the ability to fly. Hey, we'd *all* like to be Bill Gates during the week and Indiana Jones on Saturdays.

Every man knows at least one Achiever who got his ring. Confidence? Decoded. Six-figure income? Decoded. Bad breath? Decoded. Monday morning blues? Decoded. Investment and retirement plans? Decoded and decoded. Happiness, good health, nice car, par golf, gorgeous wife, and an encouraging personality that makes everyone like him? All decoded.

What if you're working with Mr. Success? How do you stand up for Christ around someone whose achievements surpass your very dreams? In some ways you wish *you* were more like *him*, and you're *sure* he wouldn't want to be like you. So what do you do?

Take heart, Brother Average. And take a look at the situation from the heavenly places where God has seated you (Ephesians 2:6). Here are the facts.

- The Lord obviously has shown grace to this man by giving him so many abilities.
- Therefore, your admiration for his *skills* may be warranted, and you may indeed stand to learn much from him.
- Your Christian witness is a gift from God to him, better than any he already possesses.
- Offering your friendship and humbling yourself to learn from him makes sharing your faith with him all the more natural and acceptable.
- The kindest, greatest, handsomest man in the world is still "dead in trespasses and sins" until Christ makes him alive.

That's reality, as seen from the heavenly places.

The biggest obstacle you're likely to face with this man is his sense of self-sufficiency. He may be humble and caring, but still possessed of a pride that says "too much" religion is a crutch.

Still he's likely, when asked, to say, "I consider myself a Christian," which is the pragmatist's variation on the what-ever-you-believe theme. Congress, not heaven, is where such people go when they die, and this *wunderkind* may already have polished the politician's favorite response to any further questions about faith. "My religion is a very deep and personal thing."

That means, "I'm pretty firm in what I think but can't explain my position, and I'd rather not discuss it with you in case I'm wrong." Sometimes, it seems, personal things are so "deep" we can't find them.

Don't be snowed by someone so good he's learned to snow himself. He doesn't have it made, and sooner or later reality or the IRS will pop the champagne bubble he calls life. In the meantime there are things you can do to help the nearly perfect come to grips with his need of Christ.

First, be quick to humbly give thanks to God for everything when you're around him, and ask him if there's anything in his life he'd like you to pray about. Successful people don't receive such offers very often, yet they need them more than the outside world would ever suspect. Once in a while a guy like this surprises you and gets honest and genuine!

Second, keep your promise and pray for the man. Ask the Lord to give you wisdom in your dealings with him (James 1:5). Then follow up by telling him you prayed. Tell him you'll keep praying until there's a change.

Third, let God demonstrate His strength in your weaknesses. Don't be intimidated by success, and don't let your own humble position in life be a muzzle. Instead, "let your light shine." Boast a little about the sufficiency of God (2 Corinthians 12:9). His "inner giant" needs to see someone who is truly happy being just the right height in Christ.

Finally, affirm the Christian qualities he may already exhibit. But also let him know that righteousness isn't a question of good versus evil, but of lordship. Who will be Lord?

This is the toughest issue for a self-motivated person to face. *Who's in charge?*

You'll know you're making progress with the Great Achiever when you hear him make one small but crucial admission that says, in so many words, "God is God and I'm not." Such is the seed that later blossoms into faith. In the meantime, pray, persevere, and try to get a few investment pointers.

Knock Knock

They are among the most dreaded of creatures ever to traverse the American sidewalk. Housewives shutter blinds and check locks. Dads mute the TV. Children are enjoined to cease all movement and noise until further notice. Don't even breathe. Maybe they'll go away.

Are we talking about street gangs? Bill collectors? No, we're talking about concrete-cruising cults. We fear letting them in the door but feel guilty turning them away. It's a no-win situation.

The question is, how are guilt and fear induced by nothing more than a couple of nice young men on bikes or a carful of old ladies who don't even know we're home? The answer is that they represent everything we don't know about the Bible. They usually have studied their heresies more than we have examined the truth.

Let me tell you right away that the doctrines of the cults are not difficult to refute. With a few simple facts, you can have these folks scrambling to get back to the temple library in no time. But Jesus has commissioned us to catch fish, not spear them. These poor souls are lost in a maze of sidewalks.

Wouldn't you really rather have the opportunity to show them the true way to God?

We'll keep our advice short and sweet (for those of you who just picked up the book and flipped right to this section because you need help NOW before they ring the bell).

First, invite them in for a cup of anything decaffeinated. (Mormons, for instance, consider caffeine an illicit drug.) Then, when you first sit down, tell them you wish to dedicate your time with them to God in a brief prayer. It's your house, so they can't object.

As you pray, just express your love and thanks to God. Remember, these folks work hard because they think that's the basis for earning God's approval. Their sense of unworthiness and inferiority is profound—it is their core motivation. They need to see and hear—probably for the first time—someone who can "approach the throne of grace with confidence . . . [to] receive mercy" because God has forgiven and redeemed him (Hebrews 4:16).

Second, ask them if they're happy attempting to serve God in this way. Is life fulfilling? Don't simply pretend concern. Show it! These are generally dedicated, unselfish, but unfulfilled people.

Third, be aware that these folks have studied severely abridged versions of the Bible, and in the case of Mormonism, have embraced additional counterfeit scriptures. Mormons will tell you that Adam eventually achieved divinity, that He became God. Thus God is a man, you'll be told, with prooftexts that speak of His eyes, ears, hands, and other parts.

But your Mormon visitors haven't considered Psalm 91:4, in which God promises to "cover you with his feathers, and under his wings you will find refuge." Nor have they processed His claim to be "a consuming fire" (Deuteronomy 4:24; Hebrews 12:29). They also have not examined the New Testament avowal that "God is spirit" (John 4:24), nor the Old Testament declaration that "God is not a man, that he should lie, nor a son of man, that he should change his mind" (Numbers 23:19).

Jehovah's Witnesses, whom you are also likely to meet at your door, believe that Jesus was originally the Archangel Michael. And they too will offer you the results of their training and careful study as proof. But that study has been conducted in a theological vacuum. Their teachers have made sure to keep their minds hermetically sealed, so they wouldn't come across troubling passages such as the first chapter of Hebrews.

> But in these last days [God] has spoken to us by his Son, whom he appointed heir of all things, and through whom he made the universe. The Son is the radiance of God's glory and the exact representation of his being, sustaining all things by his powerful word. After he had provided purification for sins, he sat down at the right hand of the Majesty in heaven. So he became as much superior to the angels as the name he has inherited is superior to theirs. For to which of the angels did God ever say, "You are my Son; today I have become your Father"? Or again, "I will be his Father, and he will be my Son"? And again, when God brings his firstborn into the world, he says, "Let all God's angels worship him" (Hebrews 1:2–6).

Hebrews was written for these folks, as though the Holy Spirit had decided to travel across time to your living room and greet them personally. Point them to verse five, which rhetorically asks the reader to name any angel God ever called His Son.

Your Watchtower Society guests also have not been exposed to the apostle Peter's statement that the Spirit of Christ testified beforehand to the sufferings of Christ and the glories that would follow . . . things that even angels desire to look into. (See 1 Peter 1:11–12.)

Both Jehovah's Witnesses and Mormon missionaries have been trained to treat challenges like these as arguments to be avoided, and have been instructed to leave as quickly as possible for their next destination. Therefore it's important for you to make your points as responses to their presentation rather than as a sermon of your own. If they stay, even for a little while longer, it's a sign of progress. And when they leave, ask them if you can pray for them as they go on their way.

The best sign of all? If they show up again, especially with a "coach." That means they have genuinely responded to your friendship and also took some very troublesome questions back to headquarters.

Just have lots of decaf ready.[2]

The Hypocritical Oath

For the past few pages, we've dealt with false religion in its various guises, each one sewn from the same fig leaf. All are equal-opportunity violations of the First Commandment, by which God prohibited other gods.

I've encouraged you to pray, to reach out with confidence, to humbly confront deception, and to fan the sparks of potential faith. Now I want to tell you about the most insidious false religion of all: *counterfeit Christianity.* No less than a demonic perversion of the Second Commandment, it shuns the worship of false gods in favor of pretending to worship the true God. Whereas modern pagans from New Agers to Mormons are given mainly to delusion, counterfeit Christians trade in pure hypocrisy. Paul warned the Corinthian Christians about them:

> But now I am writing you that you must not associate with anyone who calls himself a brother but is sexually immoral or greedy, an idolater or a slanderer, a drunkard or a swindler. With such a man do not even eat. (1 Corinthians 5:11).

The apostle didn't hedge. "Put away from yourselves that wicked person," he quoted from Deuteronomy, using the Mosaic phrase for capital punishment. Excommunication from the church was no less than a spiritual death penalty, reserved exclusively for those who wanted to lay claim to new life in Christ while deliberately continuing in sin.

So what does a spiritual execution have to do with you? Well, I'm certainly not suggesting you carry one out on your own. Vigilantes don't inherit the kingdom. But you can stand up for Christ by exposing the liar who masquerades as a follower of Jesus. That's what Dr. Greg Bahnsen did in Moscow a few years back.

I hosted the late Presbyterian scholar's first and only mission to Russia, two years before his death. His expertise in biblical law, along with his celebrated debating skills, made "Dr. B" perfectly suited to speak to educators, entrepreneurs, and government officials in the newly liberated "former" Soviet Union.

One of the initial items on our itinerary was an invitation to participate in the First Conference on Religious Liberty in Russia. As we entered the auditorium it quickly became apparent that this was not a Christian event, despite the fact that it was being chaired by a prominent Protestant leader.

After a speech by President Boris Yeltsin's official representative, in which he assured everyone that—and he actually said this—"all religions will be regulated equally in the new Russia," it was time for clergymen to take their turns on the podium.

Speaker after speaker, from bishop to maharishi, called for (a) government financial assistance, and (b) a Russia where "all religions are welcome and free." That seemed to be the slogan of the day. All religions would be equal in the new Russia. Certainly the Christian ministers present on this occasion were happy with it. All but two, that is.

Greg and I looked at each other. His neck was red and there were sparks in his eyes. I thought of Elijah and the prophets of Baal (1 Kings 18), and thanked God for the honor of serving Him in a similar setting. "Go for it," I whispered as my friend sprinted to take his turn at the microphone.

Dr. Bahnsen graciously greeted his hosts but politely moved straight to the point.

"Over and over today I have heard speakers hail the new Russia as a nation where all religions are welcome. But do you really mean this? Or do you welcome only those of which you approve?

"I look around but I don't see Satanists. Are they not welcome in the new Russia? What about the Branch Davidians, Catholic Inquisitors, Protestants who slaughtered native Americans, or militant Moslems who evangelize with the tip of the sword? Are these not welcome in the new Russia?"

On he went, calling fellow Christian ministers to task for their hypocrisy. Of course Satanists and murderers would not be welcomed. But who would be, and why? By what standard would religious freedom be measured? He held his Bible high to answer his own question. It was the only Bible that had been on the dais all day.

I had never heard the gnashing of teeth until that moment. There were murmurs, clicks, and grunts. The "peaceful" were raging at us with a quiet ferocity that seemed ready to abandon civility. Instinctively my eyes traced a path to the nearest exit. It was God's work, sure, but I wanted to be ready if His plan included an end run.

Instead, vindication came when an Orthodox priest, representing Russia's most powerful religious body, strode to the podium and echoed the American theologian's prophetic declaration. The mob was quickly subdued. Ranting at the Russian Orthodox Church was a more serious consideration.

In the meantime, Elijah and I headed back to the hotel.

The basic rule for dealing with blatantly hypocritical Christians is that you do it face-to-face. There's no way around that. But the Bible is as clear about the spirit of the confrontation as it is about the necessity of it.

First, Ephesians 4:15 prescribes "speaking the truth in love." In other words, you don't avoid the truth, but you also don't bludgeon a brother with it, even a false one. Watchman Nee, the great Chinese Bible teacher, once warned that a Christian should never enjoy issuing a rebuke. He was right. Even though Jesus flailed away with a whip when He tore through the temple (John 2), He also mourned at having to leave it desolate (Matthew 23:37–39).

Second, don't let yourself become a heresy hunter. Paul's admonition was and is to shun the counterfeit believer. Avoid his company. Don't let him pretend to be your friend. The only time to confront him is when he openly misrepresents Christ, as those religious libertines in Moscow were doing.

Finally, be prepared to help with his restoration should he repent. This will take time and should be supervised by church elders. In fact, the restoration of a brazen hypocrite *demands* time, because that's the only way for him to demonstrate a change of character.

Oh, and the sound you hear . . . that's the Father rejoicing: "For this son of mine was dead and is alive again; he was lost and is found" (Luke 15:24).

War and Praise

We have powerful, spiritual weapons for "demolishing strongholds," says 2 Corinthians 10:4. The mightiest one of all, without a doubt, is the sword of the Spirit, God's Word (Hebrews 4:12, cf. Ephesians 6:17). Knowing how to use that sword is important in standing up for Christ. Hence I've just given you a fencing lesson.

But no Christian man is fit to wield the sword of the Lord until his training is complete, and there's one more move to learn before this class is dismissed. It's from the Psalms. "May the praises of God be in their mouths and a double-edged sword in their hands" (Psalm 149:6).

Swords are dangerous, especially God's sword. Truth in the hands without praise in the mouth is an utterly deadly combination. But a tongue that sings praise to God is the tongue of a man fit for war.

So whether you're facing idols on a coffee table or in the boardroom chair, keep God's praises on your lips. As one of history's greatest warriors once said: "I will praise you, O LORD, with all my heart; before the 'gods' I will sing your praise" (Psalm 138:1).

For Thought and Discussion

1. Where do you stand on the matter of truth? Has God set standards of absolute *right* and *wrong*? Or do you suspect that "sincerely" believing in a false religion, and rejecting the Word of God, will be acceptable to God?
2. What is your attitude, or response, to the current mindset in our culture that says we are to be "tolerant" and "accepting" of all views and religions? Do you respond with irritation? Sarcasm? Or do you agree with it and go along? How could your attitude become more biblical—and more Christlike?
3. What is your attitude toward cult members who come to your door? Do you pretend you're "too busy" to talk? Shrug, and think, "They'll figure it out someday without my help"? Or cop out, saying, "I don't like to argue religion"? Why not drop the excuses and *prepare* to speak for your faith?
4. What would you do if you found yourself in a situation where another Christian was compromising the truth?

Notes

1. According to *Virtual America, The Barna Report 1994–95*, 61 percent of Americans surveyed agreed with the statement, "If a person is generally good, or does enough good things for oth-

ers during life, they (sic) will earn a place in heaven" (p. 116).

2. If you'd like to add a basic knowledge of today's cults to your coffee supply, check out *Kingdom of the Cults*, by the late Walter Martin (Minneapolis: Bethany House Publishers, 1985).

The Untouchables:
Taking a Stand With People You Dislike

Who is it that grates you? Who gets on your nerves? Maybe it's that unkempt character that's always at the stop light with the "will work for food" sign, the one who failed to show when you offered him work. Or the game-show host whose hair is so puffed and sprayed it looks like somebody stuck a grass hut on Mount Rushmore. Or that weirdo with the red, white, and blue afro who always jumps around behind home plate at baseball games with a John 3:16 banner.

"Ah, those guys are generally harmless," you say. For you, it's the wife-beaters and the scum who sell drugs to kids that make your blood boil; or militant feminists and gay-rights activists; or lying politicians on both sides of the political fence.

Maybe there's no stereotype involved, no defining characteristic that puts you off. Sometimes a person is simply irritating to you, in ways you can't explain. Just like ex-President Bush scorns broccoli, you avoid some people. Other folks might like them fine, but you don't. It's not that you hate them, they just, well . . . get on your nerves.

Will Rogers claimed he never met a man he didn't like, but I'll bet with a few he really had to work at it. In a world that's produced billions of spiritual mutants (aka sinners), it's no big surprise that some of the mutants don't like some of the others. You and I have probably been left off a few guest lists ourselves. But the fact that jocks and Jeopardy contestants don't necessarily choose to hang out with each other isn't what we want to rectify here.

What we want to tackle is how you take a stand for Christ with those people who—whether they realize it or not—push your buttons the wrong way. Your problem might be the white guy who patronizes you by constantly calling you "my main man" and trying to high-five you, instead of just shaking hands like he does with everyone else. Or you might *be* that guy. You tell yourself you're not prejudiced but have to admit that you're still uncomfortable around "certain" people at the office.

Part of standing up for Christ is loving people the way God loves them. That means learning to see them as He sees them. And a good way to start is to look at ourselves from His point of view.

Mirror, Mirror On the Wall

You and I are nice guys, right? I mean, we've got our faults, but we're not beer-guzzling jerks who slap their wives around and beat their kids. And we're certainly not madmen—like Charlie Manson or Jeffrey Dahmer.

Just today I saw a news report about a man who murdered a California teenager and then bragged about it in a letter to a friend. He was proud of what he had done.

Is hell hotter for gross offenders like these? Is there special torture reserved for them, some eternal version of the pain they inflicted during their lives on earth? If I had made hell, there would be, and you might feel the same way.

The truth is, Satan is an equal-opportunity tormentor. He doesn't discriminate on the basis of race, creed, religion, national origin, sexual preference, job preference, or seating preference. In hell there's only one section: smoking.

Let me tell you the cold, hard facts about you, me, and the aforementioned monsters in the Bible's own words.

> What shall we conclude then? Are we any better? Not at all! We have already made the charge that Jews and Gentiles alike are all under sin. As it is written: "There is no one righteous, not even one; there is no one who understands, no one who seeks God" (Romans 3:9–11).

> *All* of us have become like one who is unclean, and all our righteous acts are like filthy rags; we all shrivel up like a leaf, and like the wind our sins sweep us away" (Isaiah 64:6, emphasis added).

> As for you, you were dead in your transgressions and sins, in which you used to live when you followed the ways of this world and of the ruler of the kingdom of the air, the spirit who is now at work in those who are disobedient. *All* of us also lived among them at one time, gratifying the cravings of our sinful nature and following its desires and thoughts. Like the rest, we were by nature objects of wrath" (Ephesians 2:1–3, emphasis added).

Not a pretty picture, is it? But it's exactly what God sees when He looks at the human race. From the Dahmers and Mansons right down to the cutest cuddly baby, there's not a speck of righteousness in any of us. Each of us is conceived in sin (Psalm 51:5), and from the moment our hearts started beating they were "deceitful above all things and beyond cure" (Jeremiah 17:9). Sin is sin.

Grace is the one thing *nobody* deserves. In fact, the only way to qualify for it is to be undeserving. *Amazing Grace* composer John Newton wrote about "grace that taught my heart to fear" because he had realized the terrifying truth: The only people who receive God's grace are people who know they are not entitled to it.

But in the very next breath the former slave trader penned, "and grace my fears relieved." *That* is what makes God's grace amazing. It digs up the grave of sin we call our heart and shows us the cadaverous condition of our souls. It tries, convicts, and sentences us, takes us to the chopping block, and straps on the executioner's hood. Then, sword raised and standing over us in appalling anger, it points to the blood already on the stump, still wet and thick and crimson red. We freeze with fright. Our pulse pounds, as our own blood races to be shed. Death is upon us.

But the blade never cuts, though it still threatens us. Why? Because we weren't led here to die, but to see this terror and live. We were brought here to get a good, close-up look at Jesus' blood, to see how "God demonstrates his own love for us in this: While we were still sinners, Christ died for us" (Romans 5:8).

Has anyone ever offended us as much as we have offended God? Have tales of child abuse ever sickened us the way our sin sickens Him? No. Yet He showers us with grace, sprinkles us with sacrificial blood, raises us to life, washes us with His Word, and then *chooses* to love His new creation. And if we sin "we have one who speaks to the Father in our defense— Jesus Christ, the Righteous One" (1 John 2:1).

We are called to proclaim His praise. How can we *not* shout it from the housetops? How can we not shower everyone around us, from banker to beggar, with the news of His grace? After all, we have known the judgment of God and lived.

Pride and Prejudice

"Do nothing out of selfish ambition or vain conceit, but in humility consider others better than yourselves" (Philippians 2:3).

You and I both know there is no excuse for us, as Christian men, to purposely exclude people on the basis of personality, race, or physical condition. You know you should be reaching out to the unlovely, unlovable, the down-and-outers. So let's save some ink and not go over that again.

What you probably do not realize is just how much you have to offer, and what a payoff there is in investing yourself in society's outcasts. Who are these folks?

- *An Oklahoma pastor's wife whose husband died suddenly of a heart attack.* The church forsook her as soon as a new pastor and his wife arrived, and two years later she still had not received a single phone call of encouragement from the elders, nor from her denomination's area pastors.
- *A slick-haired, tattooed ex-addict who came to Christ five years ago.* He's at church every time the doors open but still sits alone because he lacks the social skills of his suburbanite peers.
- *The HIV-positive homosexual, forsaken by friends and shunned by anyone who discovers his dark secret.* Ripe for repentance, he's ready for the first time in years to hear the Gospel he rejected in his teens. But from whom?
- *The Down syndrome sufferer in his mid-twenties.* His elderly parents have recently become house-bound, virtually erasing his own life outside the home.

One of the prime reasons we avoid such people is our common misconception of "getting involved." We think it means sympathizing and patting hands, or staring at walls hour after hour in heavily curtained rooms that smell of urine. But nothing could be further from reality.

Take my buddy in Gainesville, Florida. That's his name: Buddy. He and several other adults with Down syndrome are members at the Rock of Gainesville, the church that threw a reception for the University of Florida's baseball team.

The folks at the Rock are even crazier about college football than they are about baseball. On game days you'll usually find at least a prayer meeting's worth of them over at Ben Hill Griffin Stadium, cheering on the mighty Florida Gators. And it's not unusual to see Buddy and his companions in the stands, sitting smack in the middle of the attractive young Generation Xers that make up the bulk of this dynamic congregation.

Why take a group of mentally retarded people to see a sport they'll never understand? That's the question behind the funny looks that trail Buddy's little group to their seats. Oh, there's the occasional smile that says, "Gee, what a nice thing to do," but for the most part a chorus line of raised eyebrows dances in their gentle wake.

The doubters are right, you know. These sweet-spirited, simple people don't understand why those helmeted protein machines down on the field line up again and again to smash into one another. But they cheer and do "the wave" with everybody else anyway, even though they're usually a ripple or two late. And do you know what they're yelling when a touchdown has brought the screaming throng to its collective feet?

"Hallelujah! Thank you, Jesus! Praise the Lord!" As far as they're concerned that's what the whole arena is shouting, because their experience with crowds is at the rousing worship services at church.

So, do their Christian brothers take these "handicapped" people to the games because they feel sorry for them? Not on your gridiron-loving life! Buddy and his friends are there because they give back in joy what they require in attention. And in their own wide-eyed way, they unconsciously remind their frenzied fellow believers that a stadium full of "smart" people howling over an inflated pig bladder is as good a place as any to praise the Lord.

The whole point of getting involved with such folks is to share blessing, not renounce it. Yes, Jesus said, "whoever finds his life will lose it, and whoever loses his life for my sake will find it" (Matthew 10:39), and some people are indeed called to live down at the shelter, deferring further reward until heaven.

But most of us are blessed with homes and jobs and happy lives. Not that we should give them up; but that we should *open* them up. The rescue mission is meant to be a temporary stop on the way back into society, not a permanent culture of its own.

The purpose of walking into the world of the afflicted is to bring them back alive. Jesus went to His grave alone, but a considerable crowd came out with Him!

Would it help the brother with Down syndrome if the whole church swore off football and spent Saturday afternoons just sitting in a room with him, "embracing" his suffering? Or is it better to take him to the game? We should ask, in fact: Was the game ever so great before we took him with us?

Buddy is waiting for your answer.

The Fisherman's Friend

All right, all right, so I hooked you. You're ready to reach out and touch someone you previously did your best to avoid, without even a telephone for protection. But there's a difference between the sweet, smiling face of a Special Olympian and the effeminacy of the guy who does your wife's hair. How do you know when to reach out and when to keep your distance?

Let's take a look at how Jesus did it—how He drew His priorities and chose His friends. And while we're at it, let's see who got on *His* nerves.

Sympathy junkies love to paint Jesus as the Prince of Pity, to claim that He didn't play favorites, that He showed equal compassion to everyone, and of course that you should too. But they're wrong. He spent much more time with some people than with others, especially His disciples. And even among the twelve, Peter, James, and John seem to have enjoyed a greater degree of His attention and guidance than the others did.

Moreover, the Savior appeared to have somewhat of a problem putting up with certain types of people. He even called some men, to their faces, a "brood of vipers" (Matthew 3:7). But in the main, those who bothered Him were not the disabled or the disgusting, the nerd and the clodhopper crowd. Not even the guttersnipes and hookers got to Him. On the contrary, He hung around with sinners and was even called a friend of tax collectors (Matthew 11:19), that bunch of bean-counting characters who served Caesar's financial interests.

Even when He was dying on the cross, Jesus seemed to hold no animosity for the soldiers who had crucified Him, nor for the bloodthirsty mob. Rather, He asked God to forgive them for this, mankind's most vicious sin in a history fraught with it.

Instead, the ones who really seemed to vex the Savior were the local Pharisees, the money-changers in the temple, and anyone else who falsely claimed to represent the true God. He seemed to prefer almost any sinner to the sort of religious hypocrite we earlier called the "counterfeit Christian" (see Chapter 8).

When you think about it, it's amazing that the Lord would keep company with any of us. After all, as the only begotten Son of God, He was a culture of One. Nobody else could possibly have anything in common with Him. Everyone, by *nature*, would be disgusting to Him.

But Jesus, as we know, was not only fully God but also fully Man. In fact, He usually referred to himself as "the Son of Man." Why? Because His Father sent Him here to have *everything* in common with us!

> For this reason he had to be made like his brothers in every way, in order that he might become a merciful and faithful high priest in service to God, and that he might make atonement for the sins of the people. Because he himself suffered when he was tempted, he is able to help those who are being tempted (Hebrews 2:17–18).

This is why Jesus gave His time to prostitutes and tax collectors. Sure, they were sinners, but they didn't pretend to be anything else. He didn't approve of their sin, but He easily related to them because He was tempted to be one of them.

The Pharisees and money-changers, however, were sinners feigning righteousness. They preened in prayer on street corners and play-acted in the temple. They were just as immoral and greedy as the others, but they positively excelled in hypocrisy. So when the Savior appeared they didn't accept Him, because only sinners needed a savior.

That was the spirit Jesus loathed. Every smarmy prayer the Pharisees offered was another kiss from Judas, every coin on the money-changers' table the profits of betrayal. They crucified Him every day, these snakes.

Jesus preferred the more honest company of fishermen, tax men, and local doctors, who were more down to earth. When a woman with a past crashed one of His dinner appointments with tears of repentance (Luke 7:37–38), the Lord accepted her praise and forgave "her many sins" (v. 47). John later identified her as Mary (John 11:2), the sister of Jesus' beloved friend, Lazarus, and told of a second instance where she did the same thing.

> Then Mary took about a pint of pure nard, an expensive perfume; she poured it on Jesus' feet and wiped his feet with her hair. And the house was filled with the fragrance of the perfume. But one of his disciples, Judas Iscariot, who was later to betray him, objected, "Why wasn't this perfume sold and the money given to the poor? It was worth a year's wages." He did not say this because he cared about the poor but because he was a thief; as keeper of the money bag, he used to help himself to what was put into it. "Leave her alone," Jesus replied. "It was meant that she should save this perfume for the day of my burial. You will always have the poor among you, but you will not always have me" (John 12:3–8).

It should be clear, then, how Jesus chose His friends. The tears of a penitent sinner moved him, while the flattery of hypocrites did not impress Him. We could follow His example in choosing ours.

Prioritize your time, as even the Master did. Do what you can do from a praise-filled heart, and don't feel guilty when you can't do more.

Every man prefers to group with others like himself. That's how cultures come to be. Sheep naturally stay with their fellow sheep because familiarity and safety are in the middle of the flock. They're merely seeking to preserve and sustain themselves.

Shepherds, however, seek out sheep—not just other shepherds or the safety of the farmhouse. Their priorities are different because their purpose is different. Shepherds work for the welfare of their sheep, and in so doing are assured that their own needs will be met by the profit that comes from being shepherds. They know that dirty jobs pay well.

I won't kid you. Touching the untouchables might get a little dirty from time to time. But the payoff is absolutely unrivaled.

The Plague

Researchers aren't sure when the first carrier of the HIV virus brought this deadly passenger to North America. For a while they thought a Canadian flight attendant was their man. But a frozen blood sample from the previously unsolved death of a male prostitute revealed that AIDS had been incubating in the population for a considerably longer time. Today they're still unsure.

One thing is certain though. Acquired Immunodeficiency Syndrome will be with us for a long time. HIV will likely show up for generations to come, unless God blesses the researchers with the greatest single advance in the history of medicine.

Some Christians argue that AIDS is God's judgment on ho-

mosexuals, and thus they do not view the current HIV epidemic—the AIDS epidemic will come later—with anything
other than disgust, and that from a distance. Others disagree
and call it nothing more than Satan's latest attack on a world
Jesus died for. They point out that calling it judgment would
mean God is contrarily blessing lesbians, since they hardly
ever contract the virus. Also, many of today's victims con-
tracted the virus through blood transfusions, accidental contact, or by being born to a mother with the virus. So who's
right?

More to the point, what should be your response to these,
the ultimate outcasts? How do you minister effectively to homosexual AIDS sufferers, since they represent the category
most repulsive to most Christian men. Sooner or later your
world will include these men—the AIDS epidemic will come.
You and I must be ready for it, because the political and med-
ical worlds aren't equipped to deal with it. There can be no
détente with "alternate lifestyles." The only answer is widespread repentance.

So what can you do?

First, don't shun the company of homosexuals. Do avoid
the one who claims to be a Christian, but practices immorality
(1 Corinthians 5:9–12).

Second, love homosexuals because God has chosen to
demonstrate His love to them, even while they are sinners (Romans 5:8). This doesn't mean He approves; He hates the sin.
But He didn't come to save those who had already overcome
their sin (as if there were any). God saves sinners!

Third, don't compromise regarding God's demand for repentance. There's a common delusion among homosexuals,
that if they are genuinely friendly, merciful, and sincere in
their emotions, then God must approve of their perversion.
Like the song says, "It can't be wrong when it feels so right."

They may claim that "God made me this way. It's natural
to me." But such an argument no more legitimizes homosexuality than it does letting a man die of a heart attack because

the disease ran in his family. To the contrary, God's Word must be considered what is truly "natural," that is, the proper order for the world. Even death is an aberration, in that God did not originally include it in His plan for man.

There are also certain steps your church can, and must, take. David Chilton has pointed out[1] that the church is a culture's spiritual and moral immune system. When she fails to reach out, that failure becomes the spiritual equivalent of AIDS in our society. Sin, with all its perversions, can run rampant. Therefore, in the church:

1. We must see that Christians are educated about the coming epidemic of full-blown AIDS and start preparing as a body to minister to AIDS sufferers seeking help.

2. We must practice the ministry of healing according to church governmental order, not haphazardly with a hundred, scattered, bedside prayers. James 5:14 makes it clear that healing authority is present where the elders gather for prayer.

3. We must thoroughly disciple those who repent, through the four-step process of teaching, rebuking, correcting, and training in righteousness (2 Timothy 3:16).[2]

Yes, You Can

A woman once approached me after I had preached at her church, asking me to pray for her to be able to forgive someone for a particular offense. I smiled at her and gently told her that I would not pray such a prayer. "Why not?" she asked with a flustered look. I explained to her that where the Bible requires us to forgive, we are not to pray about it but to do it. God never commands us to do anything without having enabled us to obey.

From time to time while reading the past few pages, you've probably thought of the "untouchables" that populate the undusted corners of your world. And you may have said to yourself that you could never reach out to someone like that.

But you can. Because God commands it. It's that simple. No pep-talk needed.

You can do this.

For Thought and Discussion

1. Who do you consider an "untouchable"? Is there an untouchable in your world? What is God's attitude toward them?
2. What would you have to give up, in terms of your "comfort zone," to begin relating to someone who makes you uneasy? How would you handle your feelings of discomfort?
3. When all is said and done, *will* you take the love and the Word of God to someone who makes you uneasy, if God has placed him or her in your life?

Notes

1. David Chilton, *Power in the Blood* (Wolgemuth and Hyatt Co.), pp. 89–90.
2. Ibid., pp. 124–129.

Leaving a Legacy:
A Witness That Will Stand the Test of Time

Okay, Noah, the show's over. We've trotted them past you, two by two, a sampling of every kind of unsaved creature you're ever likely to meet. From dads who love you to feminists who don't, from old best friends to strangers you never wanted to meet, these pages have been strewn throughout with people who all have one thing in common: They're sinners who need saving, and you've got the key to the ark.

By now you know I'm not going to try to sell you on what a blessing it's been since I turned into Supergeek and started tipping waiters with witnessing tracts that look like folded five-dollar bills. But by now you also know that waiters appreciate truly good news as much as anybody else.

You've learned what it means to stand up for Christ without freezing in the headlights of an approaching atheist, and you've found out that most of them are just compact cars with compressed-air horns anyway.

You've met Buddy, my buddy, and discovered that guys like him can turn a football game into heaven with a half-time, if you give them a chance.

All that remains is for you to read about *you*, and what you did when you finally put the book down. So let's call you "Bob" and tell your story.

Bob Carnemolla was a pretty average guy when I met him, but he'd had to work hard just to make that grade. The new husband of an old friend, he was warm but weather-beaten, as though he'd gone through two years of struggles for every one he'd actually lived. He was a guy you'd remember as having tattoos whether he had them or not, with looks that made you ask yourself if you'd moved the money off the dresser when he asked to use the rest room.

His Big Apple accent fit him perfectly; in fact, any other was inconceivable. The shiny, graying, I-need-a-haircut curls, the perpetual cigarette perched between ragged fingernails, gold caps that had outlived their enamel hosts—there were *laws* requiring men like this to be from New *Yawk.*

Bob's life in Christ had begun not too much earlier at Alcoholics Anonymous, and his leathery face revealed a happy heart. His eyes spoke forgiveness; his very grin had healing in it. But he was still the kind of guy that middle-class Christians in khaki slacks never invite to the house. Which was fine with Bob because it gave him more time to spend with alcoholics like the one he once had been.

He was the smartest uneducated man I've ever known, a sort of "street theologian." We'd sit over a cup of coffee and he'd tell me what he'd uncovered in the Bible lately, trying out a concept on me and then asking if it made sense. More often than not, he matched point for point the scholars I'd read in five-pound hardbacks full of three-dollar words. His terms were homespun and salty, but he hit the nail in question on its theological head almost every time.

I wasn't Bob's only amazed listener. He often transfixed his fellow attendees at Alcoholics Anonymous, not merely because he could expound on the spiritual nature of each of the Twelve Steps of recovery but because he exemplified a confidence and serenity that come only with the taking of what he called a thirteenth step: commitment to Christ and His transforming power. Bob took A.A. back to its explicitly Christian roots, before the name of Jesus had been replaced with a reference to a "Higher Power." He knew that God's Word, spoken in Christ's name, is where true healing resides, so he used the A.A. manual as an introduction to the Bible, upon which it was originally based.

He didn't like to mince words or waste them, his love for God's Word having given him a late appreciation for language in general. He carefully searched for the right words, and where his vocabulary might fail him, his heart never did. He didn't call people perfidious prevaricators or mendacious hedonists; he just told them that they were full of whatever they were full of, because he cared and they needed to hear it.

Bob's witnessing wasn't some program he conducted from door to door with practiced aplomb. It just came out of him wherever he was. A tenant in a neighboring apartment might call the resident handyman for a sink repair. Thirty minutes later he'd stand up in the kitchen and say, "Okay, it works. Hey, is there anything you folks need to pray about before I leave?" More often than not there was, and soon Bob would have a lot more fixed than the kitchen sink.

Jump-starting someone's car, waiting for a bus, making parking-meter change—these were the beginnings of friendships for Bob, and the first steps toward Christ for his new friends. In his mind, everything was somehow connected to knowing God. He could turn a lunchtime cup of coffee into a stranger's first communion.

During what would be his last Christmas season, Bob and I sat together in his living room in Baltimore. Pancreatic cancer had infused his smile with a grimace, but he wanted to talk about his latest plans for reaching street people. He knew dying wasn't God's invention, he said, so he planned on fully living to his very last breath. "The Lord can take me, and I'll be glad to go with Him," he said, "but I'll be kicking and fighting death all the way."

And he did. The doctors gave him three months, but he

lived six. Finally, on June 28, 1994, Bob Carnemolla, aged fifty-two, did what the Bible says Jesus did. He commended his own spirit into God's hands. This soldier walked home.

When I conducted his memorial service two days later, I listened to tributes coming from folks Bob had led, o˙ was leading, to Christ. One young man was a sober, working Christian with an intact marriage, thanks to his departed mentor. He was young and strong, not worn and wiry like Bob, but he had the accent, and the same survivor's tone of gratitude. He even used terms he obviously had learned from his hero.

Bob had coached this kid along for several months, and I knew his disciple still had a way to go. But I also knew as I watched him honor a very honorable man, that he was standing up for Christ for the first time, however wobbly, on his own. And I realized that this meant Bob was still standing too.

There were others as well. A Noah's Ark collection of saints and soon-to-be's, they remain the trophies of a former loser who couldn't afford a mantel to put them on. Such is the legacy of the man who stands for Christ. When he leaves, he may leave two or two hundred standing in the place of one. Either way it's a sight that terrifies the demons of hell.

Have you ever signed up for one of those multi-level sales positions because somebody with a calculator showed you how fast your piece of the profit-pie could grow? They tell you two cents doubled every day becomes almost eleven million dollars in a month. You sell to two, and they sell to two more, and they sell to two more, and so on, and suddenly you're Bill Gates' landlord by September.

Well, now you know why Satan wants to keep you silent, or at least keep you thinking that taking a stand for Christ is an extraordinary ministry that most guys just aren't cut out for. He doesn't mind if one Christian in a million makes a hundred thousand converts. That leaves him ahead in the race for the future. But he wants to make sure you *never* discover the exponential power that exists in making a few disciples. Because then the race is over.

Make Mine Mutton

For all His ministry to the multitudes, Jesus concentrated most of His efforts on a few men from the neighborhood. He commuted mainly on foot, stayed within a few miles of home, and accomplished the eternal without ever changing time zones.

Check the record of His deeds after the Resurrection. Although He evidently appeared to His disciples suddenly in supernatural fashion, rather than spend the time dazzling them with miracles, he exhorted them about the importance of relationships. The last chapter of John's remarkable gospel makes the point vividly.

Peter, James, and John have resumed their fishing profession. Life after the Resurrection has become quiet, even boring, and they do have to make a living, y'know. And so in a scene reminiscent of three years earlier, they trawl all night but find not a single fish in their boat.

Little do they realize that it is *they* who are about to be caught. Jesus is standing onshore nearby, preparing to reel them in to teach them one final lesson on changing the world. His bait: to repeat the miracle that caused them to follow Him in the first place.

"Have you caught anything?" calls a stranger from the shore. No, they reply, not recognizing the voice. "Cast your net on the other side," He suggests in a tantalizing hint. But not until their nets are filled to the breaking point does John realize that the man in the distance is the risen Lord, appearing to them for only the third time since His resurrection.

Peter, slow to see but swift to act, dives into the water and beats the bounty-laden boat to shore. His heart pounds with excitement. The last time Jesus did this, they left the fish behind and spent three years catching men's souls, healing bodies, even raising the dead. Now He's conquered death itself. Not even Rome can stop Him this time. Surely the kingdom of God is finally here.

But what is this resurrection power being used for when Peter crawls out of the water? Cooking. The Savior of the world is cooking fish over a simple campfire! How unexpected, how mundane, how . . . mortal. Okay, so He wants to feed us, fine. But why not just zap the fish, nuke 'em with a glowing forefinger or something, like E.T.? Ah, Peter, miracles aren't the point, and fish are not the metaphor of the day, as you are about to learn in an after-breakfast stroll with the Lord.

Today's subject is feeding sheep, something a lot more complicated than fishing. I mean, with fish there's no relationship. You just catch 'em, skin 'em, sell 'em, or eat 'em. Then you move on to other fish. But sheep you have to raise, feed, shear, teach, breed. They take time—years, not hours. And you can't just leave them. They follow you. They're more than a job; they're a life sentence!

Jesus has to tell His slow learner three times: "Peter, feed my sheep." Do what I've done for you this morning. Fishing has its place, but don't spend your whole life reeling in the net and counting converts: go on and make disciples out of them. Feed my sheep, Peter. It might sometimes be as unexciting as watching bread rise, maybe downright rural to an urban sophisticate. But it's my plan to change the world.

Be Fruitful

What does all of this mean in practical terms? That God has called you to do a smaller job than you feared but a more thorough one than you expected. It means, unless you're one of those exceptions to the rule, that your most important "mission field" will be what's called a family.

If you're married, you stand tallest for Christ when you lay down your life for your wife, loving her the way Christ loves His church (Ephesians 5:25–33). The two of you are God's original mission agency, fulfilling His original great commission to be fruitful, multiply, fill the earth, subdue it, and rule it (Genesis 1:28). That is one commandment that has never been rescinded.

Standing up for Christ means realizing that children are a blessing, not a burden, a heritage rather than a ticket to the poorhouse (Psalm 127:3–5). They bring a man greater freedom to serve God, because they extend his reach. They enable him to face the future with confidence rather than fear. They're a way of leaving something of himself standing for Christ even after he, himself, is laid to rest.

Christians in first-century Rome were so convinced of this that they made a holy calling of adopting unwanted Roman children. They rescued aborted babies, born alive but discarded outside the city walls, loving many of them back to health. This meant there were pagans with fewer children and Christians with extra children. Over a couple of centuries the impact of this wonderful trend was enormous.

Adoption gives a man the power to extend his family beyond normal limitations, and a larger family, in turn, means a greater influence in life. God gave Heman fourteen sons and three daughters "to exalt him" (1 Chronicles 25:5), which means in today's terms "to increase his power base."

Another You

If anyone ever could have justifiably felt useless, Mary's husband, Joseph, could have. After all, he was the stepfather of Jesus the Messiah, Almighty God in the flesh. What could he possibly do as a father, teacher, mentor to God?

He knew the prophecies about Jesus' greatness and divinity, and he *undoubtedly* wrestled with feelings of redundancy worse than you or I could possibly imagine. Yet he taught young Jesus to work as a carpenter, passing on the skills that the Savior needed to "earn His keep" as a man. Joseph was needed.

Whether you're married or not, a dad or not, the champions of tomorrow need you. You don't have to adopt a young man to take him under your wing. You can "mentor" him like Bob Carnemolla did, making good use of a Bible, two cups, and a lot of coffee.

Mentoring (which is what they call disciple-making these days) was described by Moses a long time ago, when he informed Israelite parents that the educational buck stopped with them, not the Promised Land Board of Education.

> These commandments that I give you today are to be upon your hearts. Impress them on your children. Talk about them when you sit at home and when you walk along the road, when you lie down and when you get up. Tie them as symbols on your hands and bind them on your foreheads. Write them on the doorframes of your houses and on your gates (Deuteronomy 6:6–9).

See that? You thought you were picking up a book about going door to door, talking to strangers about Jesus. But instead we're talking about one door—yours—and what goes on inside it with your various kinds of kids—natural, adopted, and mentored. Moses made it clear that a man's daily life is supposed to involve talking with Junior and Sissy about the finer points of God's Word—like why Israelites weren't allowed to cook both a hen and her eggs.[1]

Mentoring also involves teaching your students how to pray and how to worship God, by letting them see *you* do it! Even if you sound like a cow in a breech birth, your songs of praise will have a bigger impact on your kids than all the righteous rockers that have ever damaged their ears in order to save their souls.

In short, mentoring means getting to pass along all your good points. After a couple of generations of this kind of spiritual water-filtering, the world should be beating a path to your grandkids' door for a drink. I call it "trickle-down righteousness."

Inherit the Earth

The Lord assured Israel that they would inherit the promised land "little by little" (Exodus 23:30). Why couldn't they have it all at once? Because they were too few in number, and too inexperienced in management to inherit it any faster.

God wanted them to have children, to multiply their numbers enough to overcome the Canaanites, who in the meantime were the unwitting caretakers of their inheritance. He also wanted them to gain experience in business and ownership, gradually moving up to bigger responsibilities as they were faithful in small ones (Luke 19:17).

His plans haven't changed. The "sinner's wealth is [still] stored up for the righteous" (Proverbs 13:22). But the righteous aren't fit to lay their hands on it until they become proficient with what they already have. And according to Scripture, this doesn't happen all at once.

Perhaps the greatest lesson you can learn about standing up for Christ is that you've got time to do it right. Jesus Christ was successful in seeking and saving what Adam had lost, and that included saving history itself.

Time is not your enemy. Neither is history a losing cause from which Christians can only hope to escape. Jesus will come at the appointed time, whether relatively soon or in the distant future. But it will be to cement His victory, not to call the game because He's losing so badly.

Time and history were both redeemed by Jesus, and *both are on your side.* Therefore you can use them to your advantage. You can afford to inherit the world "little by little."

Jesus once stopped during a journey because He was tired and the day was hot. His only "plan" was to get a drink at Jacob's well. But before He left that spot, He had inherited the Samaritan woman and a little bit more of the earth.

That's how He does it. He inherits a woman at a well one day, a little man named Zacchaeus on another, and a used-up Bob Carnemolla on another. Oh, there are occasional spurts of growth—the woman brings her whole town to him, Peter's Pentecost sermon hauls in a boatload—but for the most part the Lord sends one to disciple two, and two to disciple four, and so on. He gets rich slowly.

Henry Ford didn't always own Detroit. He built his first automobile in his coal shed and accidentally invented the "garage." Later, Walt Disney started his little business in one. And the personal computer was invented in Steven Jobs' garage. Ditto for Delta Airlines and *Reader's Digest*. As for Sir Isaac Newton, he didn't even have a garage, so he hung out in the garden, by an apple tree. And the rest, as they—*boink*—say, is history.

Where should you begin your kingdom pursuits? Right where you are: in your family room, garage, backyard, by the fire, at a roadside well—wherever life is lived. Then simply love God with all your heart, soul, mind, and strength, and love your neighbor as yourself.

Hollywood gives us fictional heroes, but God makes real neighbors. They are the divine prescription for world conquest. Whether you find yourself in the Kremlin or in the kitchen, do your best work every day, with a song in your heart. Pepper your speech with a spirit of praise. Kick back when you're tired, and see who comes along. Don't be afraid to ask a Samaritan for a drink, when others wouldn't even ask him the time of day.

And let's be prepared for God—in those ordinary places on those ordinary days—to accomplish the extraordinary through plain old you and me.

For Thought and Discussion

1. What commitment to standing for Christ are you willing to make as a result of reading this book?

2. What kind of a "spiritual legacy" are you planning to leave?

Notes

1. Leaving the hen protected future egg production. Deuteronomy 22:6–7 was a conservation law.